Land of Carmel

For you, Anthony, with love and gratitude, as you celebrate your Silver Jubilee of Ordination to the priesthood.

'Mother, behold your son', 'Son, behold your mother'

And in loving memory of my own mother, IDA, who died that I might live, and who is buried at Willesborough, Kent, *sub umbra Carmeli.*

'No one has greater love than this'

Land of Carmel

The Origins and Spirituality
of
the Carmelite Order

ELIZABETH RUTH OBBARD

First published in 1999

Gracewing
2 Southern Avenue, Leominster
Herefordshire HR6 0QF

ISBN 0 85244 504 0

Typeset by Action Publishing Technology Ltd,
Gloucester GL1 1SP

Printed by MPG Books Ltd.,
Bodmin PL31 1EG

CONTENTS

	Author's note	1
	Prologue	5
1	Land of Israel – Land of Carmel	13
2	Time and Place	23
3	The Rule of St Albert	37
4	From East to West	49
5	The Spirit of Elijah	65
6	Mary – Lady of the Place	81
7	The Advent of the Nuns	99
8	Clothing and Contemplation for All	115
9	La Madre	133
10	Friar John – Mystical Doctor	149
	Epilogue	165
	Notes	175
	Bibliography	177

AUTHOR'S NOTE

In this book I have wanted to give an account of the origins and spirituality of the Carmelite Order for a general readership; therefore I have had to be selective and approach the historical background in a straightforward manner.

The facts are there, but I have avoided going into controversial scholarly disputes about Carmel's beginnings and the legendary accretions which have grown up in the course of time. Documentation is minimal and there will always be room for various interpretations.

The same could be said of Carmel's spirituality. For some, that really only comes into its own with the teaching of Teresa of Avila and John of the Cross whereas, in my opinion, we have to take into account those earlier forebears who prepared the ground and did so much to preserve and enhance the Elijan and Marian traditions upon which the Order is built and sustained. The Carmelites could be likened to a tree whose trunk has divided into two parts – those who follow the Ancient Observance and those who follow the Teresian Reform. But both draw from the same

roots, and above the division the branches intermingle and bring forth similar fruit.

I want to pay tribute here to all who have helped
me to love and understand the Order's heritage.
Above all, I reiterate my personal conviction that
Carmel is not for an elite, and that conviction has
grown with the writing of this book. Carmel is for
anyone who loves, or wants to love, Mary and her
Son – sinners and outcasts, aliens and strangers, as
well as the good and the genuinely holy. If it were not
so I could not love the Order as I do.

PROLOGUE

I was fourteen. It was June and we were having time off school for a General Election. This was the day I planned to visit Carmel. Having read the *Autobiography* of St Thérèse of Lisieux I wanted to see for myself the local Carmelite Monastery whose whereabouts I had recently discovered when the family had driven past a sign that pointed in its direction. Maybe the nuns there would have a place for me, a place where I could grow to love God and live with others who loved him. I knew little more of their life than that, apart from what I had gleaned from the story of Thérèse, and another book entitled *The Nun's Answer* which had been an account of Carmelite life in the form of a diary.

I cycled down a lane that led off the main Portsmouth road, then along a gravel track. There were a few houses dotted along the path, small, homely dwellings of farmworkers no doubt. Then the track widened and I turned into open iron gates at the bottom of a hill. A dog barked and I pedalled energetically to evade pursuit. But the hill was too steep for a bicycle. I dismounted and walked the rest of the way, looking about me curiously. There was a farmhouse ahead and to the left another small drive with a gate standing open. This must be it. I looked back over the countryside from my vantage point. It was green and tranquil. Apart from birdsong the silence was so thick I could have cut it with a knife.

I saw a small board affixed to the wooden post: 'Carmelite Monastery'. This was the Carmel of Mary, Mother of Holy Hope. At my stage of awkward adolescence I was indeed full of hope for the future but desperately shy and unsure of myself. I wheeled the bike inside and passed along an avenue of poplars. Ahead, a great double door barred entrance to casual visitors. This must mark the enclosure. Beyond I could glimpse the grey towers of a solid house. I decided I would just take a look at what I could and then turn back. Just a look was enough for me.

Suddenly the enormous gates swung back, a car appeared, and in it I glimpsed the brown habits that told me nuns were aboard. I panicked. I had not thought the sisters might go out to vote. I hurried down the drive as the car drove away, fearful that someone might interrogate me, tell me I was trespassing on private property.

But I was too slow. A tiny nun, barely up to my shoulder, came running along. She was like a little brown sparrow, all eyes and glasses and soft chirruping. Did I want anything? she enquired. I didn't like to say I had come for a look because I too wanted to be a Carmelite. I was still a schoolgirl after all, not even a Catholic yet, so I asked if I might visit the chapel. She turned aside through a small door and reappeared with a key. Then she took me behind another wall and I saw a footpath leading to an outside chapel. I knelt down in the silence. From the other side of the big grille I heard a discreet cough and the shuffling of rope soled slippers that indicated

I was not alone. I buried my head in my hands and begged the Lord to bring me here one day to stay, and I thanked Thérèse for letting me find the place.

Afterwards I was taken to the outquarters of the monastery by Sr Bernadette, where I met another extern sister. Sr Anne was as diminutive as her companion, making me feel even larger and gawkier than usual. Then I had tea and looked at some of the cards printed by the enclosed nuns under the mark of *spes sancta*, holy hope. I bought a few with the pocket money I had on me, just to reassure the extern sisters that their kindness to me had not been fruitless.

Since that first encounter I often returned to Carmel – to pray, to visit Sr Bernadette, and eventually to meet the sisters who lived inside the enclosure. I remember the first time the black shutters of the parlour swung back and behind the grille I saw the face of the prioress. She spoke to me of the Carmelite vocation. It seemed so austere, so challenging, and yet so ordinary and natural; but basically I was just relieved to see that the prioress was of normal height – in fact she was slightly taller than I was!

When I was old enough to leave home I became a Catholic and made my longed-for First Communion in Carmel's chapel, kneeling beside a candle decorated with fragrant syringa, and having a breakfast to follow, where all I can recall is a little basket of holy pictures, and butter fashioned in the shape of a lily. It was another world – the world of 'old Spain' ... and nuns ... and 'apartness'.

I wanted to enter Carmel then at seventeen, but family opposition and then other commitments intervened and my path took me far away for a time. Even so, I always thought of this Carmel as my spiritual home, a place of welcome and gentleness.

At last I decided that my heart could no longer be denied. I must go back.

By now, the familiar house on the hill was no longer. The Carmel I had known had closed for lack of vocations and amalgamated with another community in Norfolk, to me an unexplored part of England.

Again I approached with trepidation. What would I find now? Had my heart been right or was I following a mirage that would vanish on closer scrutiny?

The flat land of East Anglia, the squawking pheasants, the vast expanse of sky, passed before my searching eyes as I got closer to my destination. At last the monastery hove in sight, a great pile of grey stone and brick. Everything was calm and still, as if the very air hung unmoving over those solid walls, protecting an impenetrable silence.

My heart beat wildly. Was I mad to be taking such a step? I was walking into an unknown and untested life that I had admired from afar. Whether I was doing the right thing or not was an open question . . . Well . . . I would soon know.

It was August 15th, the feast of the Assumption. I attended Vespers outside then walked to the enclosure door. It swung open and I had a glimpse of two figures waiting to greet me. Inside I saw a square courtyard with cloisters. There were geraniums in pots and the sun was shining. The door closed and all apprehension drained away. I knew I was home: 'This is my resting place forever, here have I chosen to live.'

Adjustment was easy and difficult. Easy because I knew I belonged. Difficult because my temperament was not that of a 'contemplative'. For years it seemed as if I was in a desert. I *felt* the 'outsider' despite the fact that no one else seemed to see me as such. I was too conscious of my weaknesses, my inability to 'measure up', of having a personality that found solitude extremely difficult because I was so human and needy. I felt I would always be the 'outsider' in such an environment, a Ruth figure who had pleaded to come along with the words 'Wherever you go I will go ...' yet who basically remained the Moabite, the foreigner in a strange land 'amid the alien corn'.

And then, many years later, providence arranged that I should have the opportunity to visit Aylesford while out on a journey: Aylesford, which, in medieval times, had been the most important Carmelite house in Europe and had been rebuilt as a centre of pilgrimage in our own day.

The Friars, as the place is called, is set back from the road, beautifully restored with Kent ragstone and peg tiles. Beside the building, the river Medway glides placidly past. The pre-Reformation church is long gone, but a new sanctuary, with its prizewinning sculpture of the Glorious Virgin, makes a magnificent focal point. Everywhere is activity and bustle as great throngs make their way across the lawns or pray in one of the numerous chapels. Aylesford houses a community of friars again as it once did when the Carmelites first came to England in 1242.

There is one quiet spot outside – the Rosary Walk – reserved for prayer. It was there, before the shrine of the scapular, in which our Lady is depicted with St Simon Stock, that I understood in a new way what Carmel is really about.

On the shrine's ceramic we see Simon as an old man kneeling before Mary and holding out part of his habit to her, while she, in a most gracious and loving gesture, touches the brown cloth. The holy Child clings closely to Mary, held within her mantle as she leans towards Simon to assure him that all who wear the Carmelite habit will be blessed with her special protection. Underneath the alcove is a sealed cavity holding earth brought from Mount Carmel. In the placing of this earth and in Simon's humble gaze it was borne in on me anew that Carmel is truly the land of Mary, and in being so it is a land for everyone. It is not just for the 'fervent nun' or the 'faithful friar', much less for the mystically or ascetically gifted. It is for *everyone*, just as Israel of old was enjoined to shelter and care for those whom society would be tempted to place outside its boundaries – the very ones for whom God's Son came and for whom he cares with special predilection.

Carmel is Mary's land because, as mother, she welcomes and accepts all who come to her. The habit of her Order is for those she sings of in her *Magnificat* – the lowly, the starving, those who rely on the promises made to Abraham not because *they* are good and worthy, but because *God* is good, *God* is faithful. He wants to bring all to his house of prayer on the holy mountain.

> And the foreigners who join themselves to the
>   Lord;
> to minister to him, to love the name of the Lord
> and to be his servants ...
> These I will bring to my holy mountain,
> and make them joyful in my house of prayer;
> their burnt offerings and their sacrifices
> will be accepted on my altar;
> for my house shall be called a house of prayer for
>   all peoples.
> Thus says the Lord God, who gathers the outcasts
>   of Israel,
> I will gather others to them besides those already
>   gathered.
>
> (Is. 56:6–8)

So I did not rediscover and re-choose my vocation in an atmosphere of apartness and deep silence amidst a praying community. Instead it was amid the bustle and noise of pilgrimage, of curious excited children and a crowd of sightseers that I understood best that Mary is a mother to *all* who want to come beneath her mantle and share in her love.

The land of Carmel is for *anyone* who wants to dwell in it, for it is the land of Mary and her Son. She says with Wisdom personified:

> Like the vine I bud forth delights,
> and my blossoms become glorious and abundant fruit.
> I am the mother of beautiful love,
> of fear, of knowledge and of holy hope;
> being eternal, I am given to all my children,
> to those who are named by him.
>
> (Sirach 24:17–18)

This then is the story of Carmel and how it came to be seen as Mary's land, her special patrimony. And it can be ours too.

CHAPTER ONE

LAND OF ISRAEL – LAND OF CARMEL

Israel – *eretz Israel* – the words evoke deep resonances in the Jewish psyche. Hebrew religion, even through all the years of exile and diaspora, has been tied to the land, a land promised to Abraham in perpetuity, sign of a covenant never to be revoked.

> I will establish my covenant between me and you, and your offspring after you throughout their generations, for an everlasting covenant, to be God to you and to your offspring after you. And I will give to you and to your offspring after you, the land where you are now an alien, all the land of Canaan, for a perpetual holding; and I will be their God.
>
> (Gen. 17:7–8)

Through all the wanderings of the patriarchs there persisted the hope that the land of Canaan would be theirs; they would settle in that land and their nomadic existence would be over for ever. Through the years of slavery in Egypt the Hebrew people never ceased longing for a deliverer who would lead them to freedom, a freedom that could only be assured if they had a place of their own, a place of safety for their children, a place where they could live according to the Covenant within a just society. The Exodus, a pivotal event of Israel's history, was the story of their being led to a land that would be their own, 'flowing with milk and honey'.

> For the Lord your God is bringing you into a good land, a land flowing with streams, with springs and underground waters welling up in valleys and hills, a land of wheat and barley, of vines and fig trees and pomegranates, a land of olive trees and honey, a land where you may eat bread without scarcity, where you will lack nothing, a land where stones are iron and from whose hills you may mine copper. You will eat your fill and bless the Lord your God for the good land he has given you.
>
> (Deut. 8:7–10)

The land was not earned. It was truly 'gift', simply because God had chosen his people, nurtured them, cared for them, and would continue to do so.

> The Lord's own portion was his people,
> Jacob his allotted share.
> He sustained him in a desert, in a howling
>   wilderness waste;
> he shielded him, cared for him,
> guarded him as the apple of his eye.
> As an eagle stirs up its nest and hovers over its
>   young;
> as it spreads its wings, takes them up,
> and bears them aloft on its pinions,
> the Lord alone guided him;
> no foreign god was with him.
>
> (Deut. 39:9–12)

So Israel lives in safety, untroubled is Jacob's abode,
in a land of grain and wine,
    where the heavens drop down dew.
Happy are you O Israel! Who is like you,
a people saved by the Lord,
the shield of your help and the sword of your
    triumph.

(Deut. 33:28–29)

On the people's part there was to be fidelity to God's
choice shown by humility and gratitude. It would be
only too easy, when settled and prosperous, to forget
that the land was gift; to abrogate to themselves
powers that were not theirs by right, as if they had
acquired the land merely through their superior military strategy or political acumen. Never were the
Israelites to forget that the land was held in trust. To
dwell in it was to be obligated to a way of life that
reflected the generosity and fidelity of the One who
had gifted them. Care of the stranger, the orphan, the
widow, was enjoined because Israel knew what it
was to be weak, to be helpless, to have to depend on
others, as had happened to them during the years of
captivity in Egypt.

The journey through the desert to the Promised
Land was Israel's 'honeymoon', as later prophets saw
when they looked back:

I remember the devotion of your youth, your love
as a bride, how you followed me in the wilderness,
in a land not sown. Israel was holy to the Lord, the
first fruits of his harvest.

(Jer. 2:2–3)

Later, when the people were exiled to Babylon, the
joy of their return was reflected in the greening of the

whole countryside as it shared in the jubilation. The land then mirrored the fruitfulness of the once barren Sarah as she exulted in motherhood. The barrenness of exile and infidelity was to result in a new relationship of love and commitment between God, land and people.

> You shall no more be termed Forsaken,
> and your land shall no more be termed Desolate;
> but you shall be called My Delight Is in Her,
> and your land Married.
> For as a young man marries a young woman,
> so shall your builder marry you,
> and as the bridegroom rejoices over the bride,
> so shall your God rejoice over you.
>
> (Is. 62:4–5)

Since the destruction of the second temple by Pompey in C.E. 70, and through all the years of the Diaspora, the Jewish people longed for a land where they would once more be 'at home'. 'Next year in Jerusalem' was their wistful cry every Passover as they left the door ajar for Elijah, herald of the coming Messiah who would lead them back to Zion.

Jesus must have inherited this love for his own land, the land in which he was born and reared. He would have loved the hills of Galilee where he had grown to manhood, the walls of Jerusalem which he sighted yearly as he went to celebrate the Passover, the paths and streams with which he was familiar as he travelled around proclaiming the Kingdom of his Father. He would have seen the spring flowers suddenly burst into blossom, transforming the landscape into a riot of red and purple anemones, 'lilies of the field', clothed more magnificently than Solomon in robes of state. He would have known the pitiless

glare of the sun in the Judean desert, the vines and fig
trees that shaded the white houses from the heat, and
the people who lived there, like Martha and Mary,
who provided for his needs and listened to his
message.

The life of Jesus is made more real and immediate
when visualised against the landscape that was its
setting.

It is said above all that Israel is the land of light,
and that anyone who has seen the magnificent view
of the sun rising or setting above the Holy City, or the
solitary, translucent clouds above the Mount of
Olives, will read with new eyes the words of Isaiah:

Arise, shine, for your light has come,
and the glory of the Lord has risen upon you.
Nations shall come to your light,
and kings to the brightness of your dawn.

(Is. 6:1–3)

and understand better Jesus' claim to be the Light of
the World.

Everyone's own country is somewhere special to
them, but to the Jews the land was not only theirs, it
was the land of God. Everything about it and in it
spoke of his presence. Every custom, every familiar
way of eating, relaxing, worshipping, was given by
the One who had chosen Israel to be his. And this was
Jesus' own country too, the land where his home and
family was established in a small town called
Nazareth, where he would learn the trade of a
carpenter.

The whole of Israel is sacred to the Christian
pilgrim today because here Jesus lived and worked
and taught, suffered and died. Here we can see him
'in his place', among his own countrymen and

women. Here we know he actually walked the roads, his eyes rested on the same hills and valleys. Just as the Jewish pilgrim can visit the tombs of Abraham and Sarah in the cave of Machpeleh, Rachel's tomb in Bethlehem and the tomb of King David on Mount Zion, can look over the fields where Ruth gleaned and Jesse brought up his sons, so the Christian too can relive the whole of sacred history as it unfolds before the inner eye of anyone familiar with the Bible.

No wonder that the Holy Land has always exercised a fascination over the hearts of men and women of faith. The Incarnation, God-with-us, means that the incomprehensible God has entered into human history, at a certain point in time, as a person of a certain race and culture, among compatriots who shared a common heritage.

One hill that would have been familiar to Jesus during his Galilean boyhood and youth is that which takes the traveller up to Nazareth. From it Jesus would have been able to recapitulate his people's history as it passed before him. The plain of Esdraelon, stretching towards the hills of Samaria, had seen some twenty battles where chariots and horses from Egypt, Assyria and Babylon had engaged the Israelites in fierce combat. Here on this plain Barak had routed the Canaanites under the watchful encouragement of Deborah, a 'mother in Israel' (*cf.* Jud. 5:7), a prophetess known for her wisdom and impartiality in judgement. Here Gideon had driven back the Midianites. In these hills Philistines had joined forces against King Saul and his son Jonathan after Saul had consulted the witch of Endor, and here Josiah's body had been spirited away from the triumphant Egyptians to sorrowful burial in Jerusalem.

To the south, Samaria had known the figure of Elijah, famous for his prophetic denunciation of pagan worship. On the skyline Jesus could make out the area that had been Naboth's vineyard where Jezebel was to die. To the right, the long ridge of Carmel cut the sky, its peaks hiding the glittering sea and the promise of the great world beyond the horizon. There, men of Acre, Tyre and Sidon voyaged as far afield as Britain, trading for tin from the Cornish mines.

Carmel is not a single peak but a range of mountains, renowned since ancient times for its beauty and fertility. Mount Carmel is sixteen miles long by four or five miles wide and 1,800 feet high. Its name is derived from the Hebrew *Karem El* which means vineyards of God. In Biblical times it was covered by vines and remained green throughout the year.

Isaiah sang of the returning exiles from Babylon seeing the land transformed from a wilderness into a flourishing garden with all the beauty of Carmel, Lebanon and the plain of Sharon; whereas before, even this lovely mountain had entered into mourning, reflecting in its despoliation the sorrow of the people whose history it shared (*cf.* Is. 35:1–2, 33:9). The bride of the Song of Songs was lauded for her graciousness with the accolade 'Your head crowns you like Carmel and your flowing locks are like purple' (Song 7:5), and we can picture this 'queenly maiden' walking with the poise of those Arab and African women whose posture allows them to carry heavy waterpots on their heads with all the ease and grace of a dancer. Israel restored was to be fed on the finest pastureland of Carmel (Jer. 50:19), similar to the theme of the shepherd of Ezekiel who loves and cares for the whole flock:

I will bring them out of the peoples and gather
them from the countries and bring them into their
own land; and I will feed them on the mountains of
Israel, by the watercourses and in all the inhabited
parts of the land. I will feed them with good
pasture, and the mountain heights of Israel shall be
their pasture ... I will seek the lost and will bring
back the strayed, and I will bind up the injured,
and I will strengthen the weak.

(Ez. 34:13–16)

Carmel in its beauty is a mountain which encapsulates the goodness of the whole of *eretz Israel*, its
welcoming shade providing joy, shelter and security.

Above all, Carmel in Old Testament times was
renowned as the mountain where Elijah had
confronted the priests of Baal and triumphed through
his unwavering faith in the God of Israel. In Hebrew
mythology Carmel had been the dwelling place of
this great prophet, of his disciple Elisha to whom he
bequeathed a double share of his spirit, and of the
'sons of the prophet' who shared the Elijan charism
and bore witness to the continuing presence of the
Lord in Israel's midst.

From the earliest Christian centuries there were men
and women who wanted to visit the places hallowed
by the presence of Jesus and other Biblical figures.
Some even decided to erect hermitages for themselves
in the remoter spots connected with salvation history
and spend their lives there in prayer and meditation. It
was as if the land itself held them, exerting a magnetic
attraction. With the psalmist they 'thirsted for Zion',
could never forget Jerusalem, Bethlehem, Nazareth,
the Judean desert, Galilee, Tabor and Carmel. In ones
and twos, or even in small communities, Christians
kept alive the stories associated with the land of the

Messiah's birth. Through successive conquests, hermits of Eastern and Western origin settled in holy places, sometimes allowed to live peacefully, sometimes hounded from place to place, often persecuted or expelled. But somehow they continued. They wanted to breathe the air of Israel, feel Israel's soil beneath their bare feet, feast their eyes on the fields, lakes and mountains that Jesus had beheld during his earthly life.

And here the story of the Carmelites begins, surfacing from a seed planted far back in history but only coming to prominence during the era of the Crusades, when a group of Latin hermits made their home in the Wadi es Siah on the holy mountain of Carmel and sought a Rule from the Latin Patriarch of Jerusalem, Albert of Avogadro.

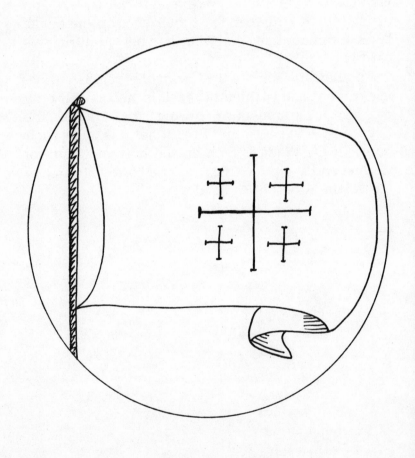

CHAPTER TWO

TIME AND PLACE

The era of the Crusades, which saw the establishment
of the Hermit Brothers on Mount Carmel, can be
dated from 1099 when Godefroy de Bouillon
marched victoriously into the church of the Holy
Sepulchre in Jerusalem, until 1291 when the last
citadel crumbled before the advance of the Moslem
troops. Midway, in 1187, came the Battle of Hattin,
when Jerusalem fell once more to Turkish
conquerors. This resulted in the inexorable pushing
back of the Christian armies, until all that was left to
them was the north of the country around Carmel
and the port of Acre. The crusading enterprise continued for a few more decades but no land was ever
permanently regained, and eventually the momen-
tum evaporated into skirmishes nearer home and the
ever present harassment of the Jews.

But while they lasted, the Crusades exercised a
fascination over the medieval mind. Indeed, the
recovery of the Holy Land, whether as symbol, ideal
or immediate duty, pervaded the mentality of two
centuries. Godefroy de Bouillon was numbered
among the Nine Worthies in company with Joshua,
David, Judas Macchabeus, Hector, Lysander, Julius

Caesar, Charlemagne and the legendary King Arthur. His exploits were celebrated by troubadours who travelled the courts of Europe singing of his deeds of chivalry and the delights of courtly love.

A man who 'took the cross' was a privileged person protected by law, and if he fulfilled his vow he obtained a plenary indulgence for the remission of his sins. He was the beneficiary of both civil and ecclesiastical bounty, admired and lauded for his sacrifical service of Christ.

Europe at this time had emerged from the Dark Ages and was almost a fully Christian society, but there were many petty kings and rulers who were constantly feuding with one another. Meanwhile Palestine had been overrun by the Saracens and travelling to Jerusalem had become a dangerous and difficult venture for the pilgrim. The popes therefore used the Crusades, not only to bring unity to disparate factions of society, but to inspire people with a renewed love for the holy places. A common cause to fight for would hopefully foster a common Christian identity. One of the offshoots of this policy was the emphasis on converting Eastern Christians encountered by armies en route to the Holy Land, culminating in the infamous sack of Constantinople in 1204.

The Crusades were able to offer men a challenge that was thought worthy of their military prowess. They also provided the opportunity for adventure and the accumulation of booty, a chance to travel abroad in search of glory rather than despoiling neighbouring estates. This issued in a new concept of the Christian fighting man who until this time had been looked upon as merely a man of violence. Now it was recognised that knighthood could be a vocation or calling. Specific standards were set for the officer class which declared that a true knight used his weapons in the service of Christ and his Church, not just by engaging the infidel in battle but by respecting women, supporting the needy and treating prisoners with fairness. Eventually, in such an atmosphere of piety, it came about that the knight received his sword at a special Mass, following on an all-night vigil before the altar. He was then presented to his liege lord and, with hands enfolded in those of his protector, the vassal swore allegiance to his prince and promised Godly conduct befitting a Christian warrior.

With such an ideal before them, soldiers were no longer expected to plunder, rape and destroy. Of course they did, for human nature remains a constant, but at least there was an ideal to live up to even if many, indeed most, fell short of it. The dark side of the Crusades surfaced, alas, in the persecution of the Jews, the 'Christ-killers' in Europe's cities, closer to hand than faraway infidels and more helpless before the onslaught of rampaging mobs than Moslem warriors.

Peter the Hermit, one of the preachers of the First Crusade, was unashamedly anti-semitic. Passions were aroused, and while, on the whole, bishops were sympathetic and tried to offer protection to the beleaguered Jews, the rabble of peasantry that accompanied the armies was too easily diverted into violence. Many Jewish communities along the Rhine were decimated by slaughter or forced Baptism. Identical bloodshed stained the path of crusading soldiers marching eastwards through Bohemia and the Byzantine Empire. The climax was reached on July 3rd 1099, when the victorious forces of Godefroy de Bouillon fought their way into Jerusalem. Those Jews who survived the preliminary massacre were driven into one of the synagogues which was then set alight, effectively ending the Jewish presence in Palestine (where they had lived relatively undisturbed under Moslem rulers) and heralding a bleak period of persecution that would continue to reverberate throughout Europe for centuries to come.

New religious Orders arose at this time in the twelfth century, all associated with Crusader ideals. First among these were the Cistercians, the 'white knights of Our Lady' who, in a contemplative mode, imitated the hardships of a disciplined military lifestyle. The Knights Templars followed – fighting men with vows of chastity and obedience. They made the defence of the Holy Land their life's vocation, and as warriors were unsurpassed for their bravery in battle. But they also amassed vast wealth upon which the French kings cast an acquisitive eye. In the four-teenth century the members of the Temple were arrested in France under the auspices of the Inquisi-tion and tortured appallingly. The Grand Master, together with Geoffrey de Charnay, recanted the damning confessions obtained under duress, but their fate was already sealed. Before the eyes of Philip the Fair and a gaping crowd they perished in a deluge of flames. Philip watched impassively, murmuring that he would have avoided their dying curses had he only had their tongues torn out before herding them towards the pyre.

With the founding of the Templars went the Knights Hospitallers, who originally had provided hospitals and hospices for travellers to Palestine and were pledged to defend pilgrims, with the sword if need be. They soon evolved into a fighting force similar to the Templars. The Teutonic knights, which were of later provenance and drawn specifically from the Germanic peoples, actually became more influential in countries such as Prussia and Lithuania, where they were granted licence to oversee the spread of Christianity in the Baltic regions.

This was the era in which Richard Coeur de Lion and his best nobles were hardly ever present in England because of the sovereign's involvement in the Crusades. When the English came marching along the road to Acre they had already heard of St George and the legends connected with his name, exalting his courage and devotion to the cause of Christ. In time they began to believe he was actually beside them, a mysterious knight mounted on a white horse with a red cross emblazoned on his surcoat, their helper in many desperate battles. It was only natural therefore that King Richard should have restored the church dedicated to the saint at Lydda and incorporated his name into the English battle cry. From there it was but a short step for St George to be proclaimed patron of the realm, dislodging the peaceful Confessor from his position of eminence. The English adopted the cross of St George as their national flag, and it has remained so to this day.

Alongside the elevation of knighthood there developed concomitantly the ideals of courtly love. This new attitude to women combined both the concept of romance and chastity. The lady of one's choice (not usually one's wife!) was seen as unattainable sexually but worthy of receiving gestures of extravagant bravery in tournaments and gallantry in behaviour. Flowers, the exchange of mementos, protestations of undying devotion, were the *sine qua non* of romance. Marriage was still too tied up with property and family alliances to be dignified with the name of love. However, the attitude to women embodied in the new outlook gradually affected the understanding of marriage. The Church began to see marriage as a

Sacrament, not merely a social contract, a way to holiness that demanded the consent of both parties for its
validity. Elizabeth of Hungary, in her marriage with
Louis, Duke of Thuringia, modelled this approach for
many. She loved her husband unashamedly and
found in the marital relationship a reflection of the
fidelity and tenderness of God himself.

On the spiritual level St Bernard infused into his
Order, the Cistercians, a new, tender element of love
for Mary. His 'battle line of brothers' venerated the
mother of God as their own 'lady' and this was to find
echoes in the spirituality of Carmel (of which more
later).

Above all, the opening up of the Holy Land gave
impetus to love for the human Christ, the God-man
who had lived and loved in historical Palestine. Lay
movements sprang up everywhere, many of whose
members were reacting against the power and pres-
tige of the monasteries and who longer for a more
simple, direct following of Jesus, untramelled by
monastic structures and grand liturgical celebrations.
Such were the hermits who came to the Holy Land in
the wake of the Crusades, some of whom eventually
settled on Mount Carmel.

Elias Friedman, the Carmelite historian, refers to
the Order's earliest direct ancestors as 'proto-
Carmelites', a term both useful and attractive, to
describe the hermits who were the precursors of
those who were to be the first Carmelites; founders,
albeit unwittingly, of an Order that would eventually
bear the name of the mountain where it orginated.

What did it mean to be a hermit in the Middle
Ages? We tend to think of hermits as people called to
live a solitary life, 'alone with the Alone', withdrawn
from all social contacts. But the first hermits of
Carmel were referred to as 'brothers', or rather

'hermit brothers', so they were not living in isolation but in some sort of group.

There were three types of hermit in this period, the majority being drawn either from the secular clergy or the laity. There were a few hermits who had once been monks and who basically remained attached to their monastery while living a more isolated life under obedience to their abbot. Most, however, were independent lay hermits who might live in a fixed place or move around – either to preserve their solitude from encroaching visitors or to perform some useful work for the community such as repairing bridges. Only men could really be itinerants, women were expected to dwell in anchorholds close to a parish church. In England two examples of hermits like these (but from a slightly later date) are Richard Rolle, who loved to 'sit singing' of the wonders of God's love, and Julian of Norwich. Richard was a wanderer, while Julian remained securely sealed within her cell at St Julian's church.

The third form of hermit living, that of the *laura*, could evolve either from monastic or independent eremiticism. It came about when a single solitary attracted disciples, or when several people gathered together for semi-solitude. The numbers in a *laura* were usually less than twelve. Each member lived in an individual hermitage and organised life according to a pattern set by a spiritual father. This form of eremiticism was especially popular in the East. Orthodoxy had never laid the stress on legal prescriptions so dear to the Latin Church; rather it encouraged personal attentiveness to the Spirit in evolving a religious lifestyle suited to the individual.

The prayer of hermits was the prayer of the psalter, not the recitation of the full Divine Office in choir as was customary among the monks and canons regular. Hermits would recite psalms from memory as they pursued their simple tasks, turning over phrases in their minds and meditating on the words of Scripture.

Although living in solitary places, for the most part forests and mountain regions, hermits were also known for their hospitality and works of mercy. They had the freedom to plan their lives around prayer while remaining available to respond to local or occasional needs.

Poverty was central to eremitical life. Hermits were expected to provide for themselves from their own resources, the chief means being manual labour. This was in direct contrast to monks whose great estates were often managed by lay servants. A hermit, at the very least, would cultivate a vegetable garden and work at simple crafts like basket making. He might keep domestic animals too. In fact, poverty was often looked upon as more important than solitude; it was a way of identifying with Christ-poor, humble and alone.

The earliest hermits known in Palestine were Byzantine hermits, which meant that they belonged to the Eastern Church. They tended to live in rock *lauras* – clusters of cells hewn out of the moutainside, or caves adapted to human habitation. The life of the *laura* was organised so that the week could be spent in solitude while Sunday was devoted to discussing matters affecting the whole group and a common celebration of the Liturgy. The hermits would then return from the weekly gathering with raw materials needed for their crafts. In this way the *laura* tempered the rigours of isolation with social intercourse, without subjecting the individual to the rigid discipline of a monastery and the full common life.

Archaeological evidence suggests that there was a Byzantine *laura* on Mount Carmel in the very place where we later find the Latin hermits, both groups living the kind of life described above.

How did Latin hermits, that is, hermits belonging to the Western form of Christianity, come to be on a former Byzantine site?

After the crusaders had taken Jerusalem in 1099 they established by degrees a Latin kingdom in Palestine. With the support of fleets from Genoa and Venice, crusaders took over the coastal cities of Haifa (1100), Arsuf and Caesarea (1101) and Acre (1104). Acre became the principal point of disembarkation for the many pilgrims who were to flock to Jerusalem, hermits included. Possibly the first hermit brothers on Carmel had arrived as crusaders or pilgrims – literally following in the footsteps of Christ – and had then wanted to stay on in the country they had come to love and revere as the birthplace of Jesus.

Crusading knights, convinced they were fighting for a sacred cause, could well be inspired to forsake warfare for religion. Indeed the behaviour of many of the soldiers was so profane that it could shock a man of genuinely high ideals, turning him to the thought of a more serious adherence to the gospel by way of peacefulness and prayer.

Other hermits and pilgrims might be in Palestine for a variety of reasons. Drawn from all classes of society, the Church did its bit to encourage pilgrimage by imposing such journeys as a form of canonical penance for serious crimes. The travelling took a man away from the scene of his sins for an extended period of time, while the hardships of the journey, with its attendant discomfort and expense, would be both punishment and incentive towards conversion. In fact the emotional atmosphere engendered on reaching the goal of a pilgrimage was expected to impart a feeling of cleansing and strength. Fellow pilgrims who were not penitents rubbed shoulders with those who were. They could be well-born folk who made this their form of foreign travel, and itineraries (travel brochures) were written to help them get the most from their sightseeing trips.

The first occidental hermits probably arrived in the Holy Land at the beginning of the twelfth century. They tended to choose a domicile in places formerly occupied by Byzantine hermits: Mount Tabor in Galilee, the Quarantera (a mountain wilderness near Jericho), beside the Jordan, in the desert of Judea. Others chose Carmel in imitation of Elijah, the reputed forerunner of monks.

In 1187, when Saladin won back much of the Holy Land at the battle of Hattin, it is possible that the numbers on Carmel were significantly increased by hermits fleeing there from other places. Carmel itself remained in Frankish hands until the definitive fall of the Latin Kingdom in 1291.

Archaeological evidence for Carmel's Latin hermits dates from the late twelfth century. Literary evidence is likewise reticent about any earlier settlement. Visits by Rabbi Benjamin of Tuleda and John Phocas to Carmel in 1165 and 1175 respectively, refer to a group of hermits gathered around a white haired priest-monk from Calabria by the cave of Elijah at the foot of the mountain. These were actually Greek hermits, known in crusader itineraries as the 'hermits of Carmel' but belonging to the monastery of St Margaret. When later another group of hermits, this time of the Latin rite, chose a *laura* further up the mountain, they were designated as Latin hermits to distinguish them from the others. So they obviously arrived after 1175.

This second group settled near the fountain of Elijah in the Wadi es Siah. Wadi means a ravine or valley dividing the mountain, while siah probably means hermitage. Access to the wadi was difficult, but it gave wide views over the sea and the Galilean hills and was in an ideal situation.

The fountain of Elijah was a ready water supply, and with the fertility of the land there would be an abundance of figs and olives for food. Many visitors speak of the superb setting which contributed to the prayer life of the solitaries. There was wood available for heating, vegetation for domestic animals, and a stream of pilgrims who would give alms to those who guarded the sanctuary. Remains of an earlier *laura* seem to have convinced the hermits that they were actually in a spot that had known an unbroken line of solitaries stretching back to the prophet Elijah himself.

These proto-Carmelites lived, worked and prayed in cells cut into the rock. Coming together once a week for Mass and discussion they followed a flexible routine of prayer, gave hospitality to pilgrims and perhaps went out from time to time for preaching or works of mercy.

Looking back on these idyllic days from a later period of history Nicholas of Narbonne could eulogise those early years as follows:

In the desert all the elements conspire to favour us. The heavens, resplendent with the stars and planets in their amazing order, bear witness by their beauty to mysteries higher still. The birds seem to assume the nature of angels, and tenderly console us with their gentle carolling. The mountains too, as Isaiah prophesied, 'drop down sweetness' incomparable upon us, and the friendly hills 'flow with milk and honey' such as is never tasted by the foolish lovers of this world. When we sing the praises of the Creator, the mountains about us, our fellow conventuals, resound with corresponding hymns of praise to the Lord, echoing back our voices and filling the air with strains of harmony as though accompanying our song upon stringed instruments. The roots in their growth, the grass in its greenness, the leafy boughs and trees, all make merry in their own way as they echo our praise; and the flowers in their loveliness, as they pour out their delicious fragrance, smile their best for the consolation of us solitaries. The sunbeams, though tongueless, speak their saving messages to us. The shady bushes rejoice to give us shelter. In short, every creature we see or hear in the desert gives us friendly refreshment and comfort. Indeed, for all their silence, they tell forth wonders, and move the interior man to give praise to the Creator – so much more wonderful than themselves.

Isaiah writes in a figure of this joy that is to be found in solitude or in the desert: 'The wilderness shall rejoice and flourish like the lily; it shall bud forth and blossom, and shall rejoice with joy and praise'. And we find in the psalms: 'The beautiful places of the wilderness shall grow lush, and the hills shall be girded with joy'.[1]

CHAPTER THREE

THE RULE OF ST ALBERT

The hermit brothers continued to live on Mount Carmel according to the pattern of a *laura* for some time. They were a group of men, international in origin, most likely drawn from every strata of society. There would be a few knights of gentle, even noble birth, pilgrims in the mode of a medieval Benedict Joseph Labre, former wanderers like the 'broken-backed Richard' who accompanied Margery Kempe on her travels, hermits who had lived elsewhere and were now driven to Carmel by Moslem persecution, clerics from other Orders who had elected to follow an eremitical calling, converted criminals ... There were Frenchmen, Englishmen, men from Cyprus, Sicily, the Holy Roman Empire, Brittany. All were of mature age. Their only formation was actually living in solitude, their spiritual welfare assured by those already tested who were prepared to pass on what they had learned through experience.

Sometime early in the thirteenth century, one of the group (B. is the only terminology by which we know him, although later legend has given him the name of Brocard), seems to have been the unofficial leader and focus of unity. This was obviously the moment to set the life on a more official footing and so the hermits approached Albert Avogadro, the Latin Patriach of Jerusalem, and asked for a Rule. They were ready for formal recognition as a community of solitaries.

We can only date the giving of the Rule in that it was issued during the patriarchate of Albert. He was elected to the office in 1205 and his position was ratified by the pope, who also appointed him papal legate to the Holy Land. In 1206 Albert reached Palestine, but as Jerusalem was still held by the Moslems he took up residence in Acre, across the bay from Mount Carmel. Acre had been made the provisional capital of the Latin Kingdom and was to remain so until its final dissolution. It was in his capacity as Patriarch that the hermit brothers applied to Albert for a Rule to fit their specific situation.

It is possible that Albert had already visited the brothers. Their way of life would in any case have been familiar to him because of the popularity of the eremitical vocation in Europe at that time. Albert also had a knowledge of other religious Rules which would stand him in good stead as he faced his new task. He himself was a canon of the Holy Cross of Mortara, following the Rule of St Augustine. In 1194, as bishop of Vercelli, he had drawn up statutes for canons of a collegiate church in Biella. Then just five years before coming to his present appointment he had been one of the counsellors charged with compiling a Rule for the Humiliati (a new religious Order dedicated to a life of penance).

In drawing up a Rule for the hermits on Mount Carmel Albert therefore had some previous expertise to rely on. He writes, he says in his missive, in response to a request from B. and phrases his reply in the form of a letter. Certain points of the Rule he proposes reflect the Rule of St Augustine; there is also reference to Cassian and St Jerome, but by far the predominant element is Scripture. It is a fluid and flexible Rule which has proved its adaptability over the centuries.

Albert did not consider himself to be legislating for an Order. He had in mind a specific group resident in a specific place. The hermits were not religious in the canonical sense but merely a community of *conversi*, men who were 'converts' to a dedicated life and who had renounced secular pursuits for the sake of following Christ more closely in prayer and solitude. As *conversi* they still did not enjoy the rights and privileges of monks or canons regular, that was reserved for those who followed either the Rule of St Augustine for canons, or of St Benedict for monks in the West, St Basil in the East.

Albert's Rule contains all that we would expect for hermits: solitude, silence, the prayer of the psalter, poverty, a weekly meeting, direct imitation of Christ. But it also contains community elements proper to a cenobitic life: the prior and obedience, daily Eucharist, and the provision for correction and discipline.

The original rule, as far as we know it, reads as follows.

Albert, called by God's favour to be Patriarch of the church of Jerusalem, bids health in the Lord and the blessing of the Holy Spirit to his beloved sons in Christ, B. and the other hermits under obedience to him, who live near the spring on Mount Carmel.

Many and varied are the ways in which our saintly forefathers laid down how everyone, whatever his station or the kind of life he has chosen, should live a life of alle-

giance to Jesus Christ – how, pure in heart and steadfast in conscience, he must be unswerving in the service of his Master. It is to me, however, that you have come for a rule of life in keeping with your avowed purpose, a rule you may hold fast to henceforward; and therefore:

The first thing I require is for you to have a prior, one of yourselves, who is to be chosen for the office by common consent, or that of the greater and maturer part of you. Each of the others must promise him obedience – of which, once promised, he must try to make his deeds the true reflection.

Next, each of you is to have a separate cell, situated as the land you propose to occupy may dictate, and allotted by disposition of the prior, with the agreement of the other brothers, or the more mature among them.

None of the brothers is to occupy a cell other than the one allotted to him or to exchange cells with another without leave of whoever is prior at the time.

The prior's cell shall stand near the entrance to your property, so that he may be the first to meet those who approach, and whatever has to be done in consequence may all be carried out as he may decide and order.

Each one of you is to stay in his own cell or nearby, pondering the Lord's law day and night and keeping watch at his prayers, unless attending to some other duty.

Those who know their letters and how to read the psalms should, for each of the hours, say those our holy forefathers laid down and the approved custom of the church appoints for that hour. Those who do not know their letters shall say 25 Our Fathers for the night office, except on Sundays and solemnities when that number shall be doubled so that the Our Father is said 50 times.

The same prayer must be said 7 times in the morning and 7 times, too, for each of the other hours, except for Vespers when it must be said 15 times.

None of the brothers must lay claim to anything as his own, but your property is to be held in common; and of such things as the Lord has given you each is to receive from the prior – that is, the man he appoints for the purpose – whatever befits his age and needs. However, as I have said, each one of you is to stay in his own allotted cell, and live, by himself, on what is given out to him.

An oratory should be built as conveniently as possible among the cells where, if it can be done without difficulty, you are to gather each morning to hear Mass.

On Sundays, too, or other days if necessary, you should discuss matters of discipline and your spiritual welfare; and on this occasion the indiscretions and failings of the brothers, if any be found at fault, should be lovingly corrected.

You are to fast every day except Sundays, from the feast of the Exaltation of the Holy Cross until Easter Day, unless bodily sickness or feebleness, or some other good reason, demand a dispensation from the fast; for necessity overrides every law.

You are always to abstain from meat, unless it has to be eaten as a remedy for sickness or great feebleness.

Since man's life on earth is a time of trial, and all who live devotedly in Christ must undergo persecution, and the devil your foe is on the prowl like a roaring lion looking for prey to devour, you must use every care to clothe yourselves in God's armour so that you may be ready to withstand the enemy's ambush. Your loins are to be girt with chastity, your breast fortified with holy meditation, for, as Scripture has it, holy meditation will save you. Put on holiness as your breastplate and it will enable you to love the Lord your God with all your heart and soul and strength, and your neighbour as yourself. Faith must be your shield on all occasions and with it you will be able to quench all the flaming missiles of the wicked one; there can be no pleasing God without faith (and the victory lies in your faith). On your head set the helmet of salvation, and so be sure of deliverance by our only Saviour, who sets his own free from their sins. The sword of the Spirit, the word of God, must abound in your mouths and hearts. Let all you do have the Lord's word for accompaniment.

You must give yourselves to work of some kind, so that the devil may always find you busy; no idleness on your part must give him the chance to pierce the defences of your soul. In this respect you have both the teaching and the example of Saint Paul the apostle, into whose mouth Christ put his own words. God made him preacher and teacher of truth to the nations; with him as your leader you cannot go astray. We lived among you, he said, labouring and weary, toiling night and day so as not to be a burden to any of you; not because we had no power to do otherwise, but so as to give you, in our own selves, an example you might imitate. For the charge we gave you when we were with you was this: that whoever is not willing to work should not be allowed to eat either. For we have heard that there are certain restless idlers among you. We charge people of this kind, and implore them in the name of our Lord Jesus Christ, that they earn their own bread by silent toil. This is the way of holiness and goodness, see that you follow it.

The apostle would have us keep silence, for in silence he tells us to work. As the prophet also makes known to us: Silence is the way to foster holiness. Elsewhere he says: Your strength will lie in silence and hope. For this reason I lay down that you are to keep silence from Vespers until Terce the next day, unless some necessary or good reason, or the prior's permission, should break the silence. At other times, although you need not keep silence so strictly, be careful not to indulge in a great deal of talk, for as Scripture has it – and experience teaches us no less – sin will not be wanting where there is much talk, and he who is careless in speech will come to harm; and elsewhere: The use of many words brings harm to the speaker's soul. And our Lord says in the Gospel: Every rash word uttered will have to be accounted for on judgement day. Make a balance, then, each of you, to weigh his words in; keep a tight rein on your mouths, lest you stumble and fall in speech, and your fall be irreparable and prove mortal. Like the prophet; Watch your step lest your tongue give offence, and employ every care in keeping silent, which is the way to foster holiness.

You brother B. and whoever may succeed you as prior, must always keep in mind and put into practice what our Lord said in the Gospel: Whoever has a mind to become a leader among you must make himself a servant to the rest, and whichever of you would be first must become your bondsman.

You other brothers, too, hold your prior in humble reverence, your minds not on him but on Christ who has placed him over you, and who, to those who rule the churches, addressed these words: Whoever pays heed to you pays heed to me, and whoever treats you with dishonour dishonours me. If you remain so minded you will not be found guilty of contempt, but will merit eternal life as fit reward for your obedience.

Here then are a few points I have written down to provide you with a standard of conduct to live up to; but our Lord at his second coming will reward anyone who does more than he is obliged to do. See that the bounds of common sense are not exceeded, however, for common sense is the guide of the virtues.

The phrasing of the Rule in terms of a 'life of allegiance to Jesus Christ' draws on the knightly terminology proper to the thirteenth century; the reference is to feudal military service transferred to a religious context. However, it makes clear that *all* are called to this allegiance, though there are different ways of interpreting it according to different vocations in the church. Purity of heart and steadfastness of conscience are incumbent upon all. Other feudal elements are found in the exhortation to be clothed in God's armour: the shield of faith, the helmet of salvation, the sword of the Spirit, all terms familiar to a knight of the period.

Albert legislates for a prior to be elected, so presumably B. only held a position of honour. Now it is to be formalised by vote and a promise of obedience from the rest. This is the one vow incumbent on the hermits, only later were the vows of poverty and chastity added. Each brother is to have his own cell where he prays, eats and works alone; and to discourage too many visitors the prior is to have a cell near the entrance to the property so that he can decide whether or not a person is to be admitted. Obviously one of his major responsibilities is to safeguard the solitude of the rest. One brother is delegated to attend to material needs so that none will have to worry about their material sustenance.

The kernel of the Rule has always been accepted as the exhortation 'each one of you is to stay in his cell or nearby, pondering the Lord's law day and night and keeping watch at his prayers'. Love for Scripture, continual meditation, are at the heart of the Carmelite vocation, no matter what form it takes.

Among the cenobitical requirements of the Rule is the obligation of a daily Eucharist. For this purpose Albert proposes the building of an oratory; before this the hermits had probably worshipped together in a two-roomed grotto. Now they erect a chapel, described in a thirteenth-century pilgrim itinerary as a 'little church to our Lady'. This dedication of the first church to Mary, indicating that she was the 'lady of the place', is the origin of the Order's Marian orientation, not surprising when we consider that the hermits were not monks but very ordinary people who, like Mary, wished to live a simple, Nazareth-like life, their focus being to keep and ponder the Lord's law just as Mary 'pondered all these things in her heart' (*cf.* Lk. 2:19, 51) while attending meanwhile to the duties incumbent on her as a Jewish wife and mother.

Albert gave the Rule to the brothers of Carmel sometime between his arrival in Palestine in 1206 and his death in 1214, when he was murdered during an ecclesiastical procession on the feast of the Holy Cross. His murderer was no common criminal but the Master of the Hospital of the Holy Spirit whom Albert had rebuked and deposed for immorality.

In 1215, a year after Albert's assassination, the 4th Lateran Council forbade the foundation of all further religious bodies in an attempt to stem the proliferation of groups surfacing in the wake of the mendicant Orders in Europe. All new communities, it declared, were to adopt either the Rule of St Benedict, St Basil or St Augustine. The Franciscans managed to get their own Rule accepted on the assurance of St Francis that the Pope had verbally approved it when Francis had visited him in person. The Dominicans were not so fortunate and found themselves with the Augustinian Rule interpreted by their own Constitutions. But what of the Carmelites? Their Rule had predated the Council; was it acceptable or would they, like the Dominicans, be forced to accept another? In their uncertainty they appealed to the Holy See and on January 30th 1226 Pope Honorius III approved their legislation, imposing it on the brothers 'for the remission of their sins'. However, this was still not full recognition, it merely implied that following Albert's Rule was a way of gaining a plenary indulgence; it did not convey religious status on the hermits or enable them to count themselves as a fully approved Order.

Only by dint of perseverance in further requests for clarification were the brothers eventually recognised as a valid religious foundation. After this they were left to follow their own way of life without threat of being disbanded. The Rule of St Albert has since become one of the few Rules of the universal Church, and it has proved itself by its wisdom and flexibility.

Meanwhile, the brothers on Mount Carmel were experiencing difficulty in maintaining themselves on the material level, for as Moslem influence increased, pilgrims decreased. Their source of revenue and their source of vocations were in jeopardy, not to mention the fact that, as Christians identified with an occupying army, their own safety depended on the Latin Kingdom holding out against the Turks. It was time to seek a foothold in Europe so that the community would be assured of a future.

A letter recommending the brothers of Carmel to European bishops states that 'in the silence of the wadi they prayed for the success of the crusader armies, distributed money received from abroad, and rendered a humble but indispensable service to pilgrims'. Now it was their turn to seek alms from others as they began to leave Carmel for the West.

The first foundation outside the Holy Land is usually accepted as being in Cyprus in 1240, Sicily and England followed in 1242 and Provence in 1244. Presumably the brothers departed in groups according to nationality in the hope of finding a welcome among their fellow countrymen and women.

It must have been with some trepidation that the first contingent left the holy mountain. What would they do when they reached the homelands they had left so long ago? They brought with them a tradition of prayer, of solitude, of love for Christ and his mother, and a reverence for Elijah the prophet, who had hallowed the mountain of Carmel and continued to inspire them in their search for God. As an Order the Carmelites would continue to remember their Eastern roots long after the last of the brothers had left Palestine at the definitive fall of the Latin Kingdom in 1291. They persisted in celebrating the liturgy according to the Frankish-Palestinian Rite of the Holy Sepulchre and to venerate their forebears, the first hermits, who they associated closely with the biblical prophets in spirit and legend.

But Carmel's development and increase lay in the West. Could it adapt sufficiently to meet the new challenges that confronted the men in striped mantles who, looking as if they had stepped straight out of an Eastern bazaar, were setting out on a journey that would take them far away, along new paths and into an unknown future?

CHAPTER FOUR

FROM EAST TO WEST

The brothers who left Mount Carmel to return to their countries of origin found a society permeated at every level by changes wrought by the Crusades, and dominated by the Franciscan and Dominican Orders which had arisen in response to the needs of a society in flux.

In the wake of the Christian armies the twelfth century had witnessed an upsurge in trade. Silks, furs, fine fabrics, spices, gems, perfumes, precious manuscripts, relics, were transported by entrepreneurs along new trade routes. Towns increased rapidly in size and commercial importance. Men became rich through personal industry and enterprise in a way previously unknown when wealth was tied to land and heredity. Money, not barter in kind, became the usual way of transacting business.

Former landowners, rich merchants, travelling salesmen and a vast mass of uprooted peasantry flowed into the burgeoning cities. There, lacking their accustomed sense of stability and oneness with soil and seasons, they reverted to the ever present temptation to eschew spiritual values in favour of the restless pursuit of money, or at least daily bread.

Many poor folk – *minores* – newly liberated from bonded serfdom, crammed themselves into living quarters of squalor and misery. They were vulnerable to diseases imported from the East, previously unknown and therefore untreatable in the West. Hospitals, where these existed, overflowed with inmates exhibiting the worst kinds of fevers, sores and running wounds.

Concommitantly, the established monastic Orders (apart from the Cistercians) had lost their ascendant influence. Their elaborate liturgies, fine vestments, trappings of abbatial splendour and feudal organisation meant they had lost touch with the urban masses. The monks epitomised a stable, ordered, landed society that had little to say to the townspeople, especially the poorest, to whom they appeared irrelevant and anachronistic.

Who then would instruct the common people? Who would assure them that God cared for them in their plight? They knew religion primarily in its outward ceremonial only, celebrated in an incomprehensible language. Could there be a God who was close and compassionate to them?

Francis of Assisi, born in 1181, was the greatest religious figure of the thirteenth century as the church grappled with the new situation. Son of a man who belonged to the *nouveaux riches* merchant class, and known for his extravagant lifestyle, Francis experienced a conversion that put him in touch with the Christ of the Gospels – Christ poor, humble, naked and needy. Those who followed Francis' example were to be *minores* – poor with the poor – not *majores* – like the rich. They were to live close to the people, earn their own bread or beg their way if necessary. Much of what the freelance hermits were trying to do was put into a community shape by Francis. His contemporary, St Dominic, followed a similar pattern but concentrated on preaching and study as a means of reaching the populace and combating error.

Thus there arose a new form of religious life which contrasted with the stable monastic one. It was the way of mendicancy (begging) which involved travelling, preaching, ministering directly to human need wherever people were, rather than waiting for people to come to the monasteries. It meant going into leper hospitals and hovels as well as churches. It was a life of witness that came closest to that described in the Gospels, where the apostles travelled round with their Master, doing good to everyone. Hence the terminology that prevailed – the 'apostolic life'. St Francis himself was powerfully attracted to the eremitical way, and from time to time would withdraw into solitude, even writing a short Rule for hermit-brothers of his own Order. In this he reflected the parallel tendency of the age – that of personal devotion to the human Jesus, the poor man of Nazareth, and exposure to him in silent prayer and meditation.

The mendicants viewed poverty, not just as conforming a person to Christ's poor by material deprivation. Part of poverty lay in availability. The brothers could not count on a settled lifestyle in one place; instead they evolved a system of centralised government which enabled personnel to be moved rapidly to wherever the need was most pressing.

The mendicants had no estates to administer and therefore no feudal privileges to protect. They tended to reside in small houses within towns, providing for their own needs by offering spiritual services to the populace – Masses, burials, confessions – besides practising a trade, teaching, nursing or meeting other social demands.

The friars (or 'brothers') as the mendicants were called, also stressed equality among themselves. It was of no advantage to be of noble birth when that could not obtain for anyone who joined them an abbey to govern or personal servants to attend to their needs. Instead, all were equal, whatever their social status. Officials were elected by their brethren and held office for a specified time, not for life. Superiors were chosen to do a certain job and when it was completed or they became incapacitated they returned to the ranks.

The mendicants were the first to introduce the breviary, so called because it was a shortened form of the Divine Office. As it could be contained in a smallish book it could be carried while travelling, in contrast to the great tomes in use in a Benedictine choir.

In bringing religion to the people as a service, the friars did much to popularise devotions that have continued to the present day. They wanted to make the faith comprehensible in ways that impinged on daily life. St Francis, for example, is credited with erecting the first Christmas crib by re-enacting the Bethlehem story in a cave at Greccio. Later Franciscans did much to propagate devotion in various ways to the crib, the cross and the Eucharist; to the human Christ who came to earth as a tiny baby 'helpless and hung upon a human breast', a wounded and crucified man, a God who was at our service as Food. The Stations of the Cross and the Angelus originated with the Franciscans, while the Dominicans favoured the rosary. In time the Carmelites followed with confraternities of our Lady and the scapular devotion, just as the Servites concentrated on the seven sorrows of Mary. Each mendicant Order deliberately involved the laity in some way, fostering prayer in an incarnational manner, seeing God as close and homely through Jesus and his mother; and the people responded accordingly.

When the Carmelites first came to Europe they found that they fitted neither into the settled monastic pattern of the Benedictines and Cistercians, nor yet into the mobile mode of the Franciscans and Dominicans.

The chronicles of William of Sandwich, describing the arrival of a group of 'hermit brothers' in England, stated that they travelled with Sir John Vesey and Sir Richard de Grey, returning crusaders. After being presented to the pious King Henry III at Westminster they traditionally divided into four groups, one going to Bradmer in Norfolk, one to Newenden near Hastings, one to Hulne in Northumberland, and one to Aylesford in Kent. That the brothers were numerous enough to erect four houses in England alone shows that they must have increased numerically in the Holy Land. If nothing else they needed to expand westwards for space in Palestine was limited and precariously held.

What then were the brothers to do in these English houses? Hulne remained a contemplative foundation always, as did a few in other countries when built in remote situations, but this was not possible for all. For one thing, how would the hermits support themselves? They were on no hallowed pilgrim route, they had no established tradition, and their strange habits excited ridicule. Alms were already being given to the Franciscans and Dominicans who provided a service of preaching and works of mercy, while the Carmelites provided nothing tangible.

The struggle to survive and carve out a niche for themselves is reflected in papal documents of the time. Bishops are asked to welcome the 'hermit brothers of St Mary of Mount Carmel' to their dioceses.

Permission is given for them to have a bell to summon people to worship, a cemetery to bury the dead. The bell is significant in that it was a means of drawing attention to their presence in an area, and it also indicates that the brothers were already carrying out public worship rather than just reciting the psalter in the privacy of their cells.

It has been suggested that the Carmelites might have done better to embrace a Carthusian mode of life, but this would hardly seem a possible choice when the facts are viewed impartially. By Rule the brothers were forbidden to own and farm land. They came from a tradition that had sprung up in direct contrast to that of the feudal monasteries, one which stressed simplicity, freedom and closeness to ordinary life. The Carthusians, for all their solitude, lived by a highly structured timetable with heavy emphasis on vocal prayer. Above all, the Carthusian Order needed large endowments to support the 'prayerful leisure' of the choir monks, whereas the hermits had always emphasised manual labour and poverty.

The Brothers of Carmel, then, needed time to discern what their way forward would be, but they could not delay too long. A definite decision was imperative. If they could not adapt to their new situation they would die out, and possible benefactors be discouraged from giving to an anachronistic Order out of touch with the times.

It shows what an important house Aylesford had become in that the first ever General Chapter of the Order was held there at Pentecost in 1247. Records are scarce but it would seem that the prior of the Mount Carmel community, a certain Godfrey, was elected as first Prior General. The brothers forthwith proceeded to request some changes in the Rule, which Pope Innocent IV confided to Dominican assessors.

Later that year, in a letter addressed to the 'Prior and hermit brothers of the Order of Mount Carmel' the pope approved the following changes which effectively allied the Carmelites with the mendicant friars rather than the monks, thus confirming them in their new orientation.

In the revised Rule, after the promise of obedience to the prior, vows of chastity and poverty were added. This meant that the Carmelites now took the three vows proper to the Franciscans and Dominicans rather than the Benedictine promises of obedience, stability and conversion of manners.

A clause was inserted to permit foundations 'in solitary places or where you are given a site suitable and convenient for the observance proper to your Order'. The judgement of the site is left to the brothers themselves. They are not confined to solitary places provided a life of prayer is preserved.

Meals are to be eaten in common, not alone, with the accompaniment of reading from Scripture.

The Office is to be said in choir after the general conventual usage of the time by those who can read, while the non-literate retain the saying of a set number of Our Fathers instead.

It is permitted to keep asses and mules (presumably to facilitate travelling) and poultry for eggs.

The law of abstinence from meat is also adjusted to accommodate travellers (including seafarers), while the period of night silence is slightly shortened: Compline to Prime (approximately 10 p.m. to 7 a.m.) instead of Vespers to Terce (6 p.m. to 9 a.m.).

The 'Innocentian Rule' which is the one followed by all Carmelites today, may not seem very different in essentials from Albert's original missive; but the changes were sufficient to make possible the integration of the Carmelites into the European religious scene and preserve the Order for posterity. If the brothers had refused to adapt in any way they would have faded out – an insignificant plant imported from the Holy Land which, uprooted from its native soil, simply perished. Fortunately this was not the case.

The approval of the new Rule by the bull *Quae honorem causa* in 1247 marks a watershed in Carmel's history. With it the Rule not only attains canonical status but Carmel is recognised as an Order. The legislation reflects the tendency to increased cenobitism permeating all the mendicant friars. Henceforth buildings would be on the lines of a regular conventual groundplan. Rather than a simple house or group of hermitages, a common refectory, chapel, choir and cloisters became the norm. The Constitutions still insisted on individual cells, not an open dormitory, but otherwise Carmelite houses had little to distinguish them from those of other mendicants. Even in the wadi the Carmelites were building a fine monastery, so grand that funds were not forthcoming to complete it and indulgences were offered to those who helped with the work. Excavations on site have revealed two graves in the church there – one containing the skeleton of an old man (presumed to be B.) and another the bones of a man and a woman, possibly the principal benefactors of the new building. But, as has been said, the last Carmelites were forced to leave the holy mountain by 1292 and the sumptuous edifice fell into ruins. Although the brothers continued to value their Eastern origins they no longer retained a foothold in Palestine.

St Simon Stock, an Englishman who until recently was presumed to be the Prior General responsible for the Aylesford Chapter decisions, is still revered for his sanctity even though we can discover very little about him. He may have succeeded Godfrey as

General or he may have been delegated to implement
the Chapter decisions in Northern Europe while
Godfrey returned to Mount Carmel.

Simon was certainly a native of Kent, a contemplative known for his devotion to our Lady. The ancient
Carmelite hymn *Flos Carmeli* is attributed to him, and
this song, with its haunting plainchant melody when
sung in Latin, has remained the special Marian
antiphon proper to the Order:

> Flower of Carmel, vine with blossom weighed,
> Shining light of heaven, bearing child though maid,
> None like to thee.
>
> Mother most tender, whom no man didst know,
> On all Carmel's children thy favour bestow,
> Star of the sea.

In a much later legend, preserved in a medieval
sculpture in the present Aylesford priory, it is
recounted how our Lady appeared to Simon and,
touching the part of his habit known as the scapular,
promised that she would take under her protection
all who wore a similar garment in her honour.

Underlying this story is the insight that Carmel,
from the first, considered itself as dedicated to the
Virgin in a special way. It was her own Order, her
own habit, so Carmelites could trust unreservedly in
Mary's patronage. Even in England Mary remained
'lady of the place'. She was thus blessing the brothers
as they formally became mendicants.

Simon reputedly died at a great age while on a visi-
tation to Bordeaux. His relics were venerated there
almost immediately, though his skull is now
enshrined at Aylesford. He stands for the generations
of nameless early Carmelites who were faithful

through the long period of change and adaptation; clinging to the belief that their Order would continue, trusting in Mary's protection not just in the fervour of youth but on into old age. Simon embodies this truth, content to remain anonymous with regard to his personal achievements.

As mendicants, close to the people while retaining their orientation to contemplation, the Carmelites began to make further foundations. Gradually they moved into towns where they received the right to hear confessions, to preach, to bury lay men and women in their cemeteries; all ways in which revenue could be obtained. The universities were also developing at this time and attracted communities from all the new Orders. The Franciscans and Dominicans were prominent as teachers – Albertus Magnus, Thomas Aquinas, Bonaventure, Duns Scotus are almost household names, but the Carmelites also found a more modest niche in the academic world. The universities provided an education for those wishing to be ordained and were a source of vocations from among the students. If the Carmelites were to be involved in preaching and teaching then it was imperative that they study as well as pray.

However, not everyone was happy with the turn of events. Nicholas of Narbonne, Prior General from 1266–1271 issued a denunciatory pamphlet *The Flaming Arrow* in which he fulminates against those who have thrown themselves into an apostolic life for which Nicholas deems them unprepared and untrained. He does not condemn the apostolic life as such (he mentions himself that the early hermits on Carmel had been of service to others by sharing the fruits of contemplation with them) but he does want to recall the Carmelites to their solitary roots on the holy mountain, symbol of the heights to which they are bound to aspire:

> To the solitude of the mountain did Abraham, unwavering in faith and discerning the issue from afar in hope, ascend at the Lord's command, ready for obedience's sake to sacrifice Isaac his son; under which mystery the passion of Christ – the true Isaac – lies hidden.
>
> To the solitude of the mountain was it also that Abraham's nephew, Lot, was told to flee for his life in haste from Sodom.
>
> In the solitude of Mount Sinai was the Law given to Moses, and there was he so clothed with light that when he came down from the mountain no one could look upon the brightness of his face.
>
> In the solitude of Mary's chamber, as she conversed with Gabriel, was the Word of the Father Most High in very truth made flesh ...
>
> To the solitude of the mountain or desert it was that our Saviour retired when he desired to pray; although we read that he came down from the mountain when he wished to preach to the people or manifest his works.
>
> He who planted our fathers in the solitude of the mountain thus gave himself to them and their successors as a model, and desiring them to write down his deeds, which are never empty of mystical meaning, as an example.
>
> It was this rule of our Saviour, a rule of utmost holiness, that some of our predecessors followed of old. They tarried long in the solitude of the desert, conscious of their own imperfections. Sometimes, however, though rarely, they came down from their desert, anxious so as to not fail in what they regarded as their duty to be of service to their

neighbours, and sowed broadcast of the grain, threshed out in preaching, that they had so sweetly reaped in solitude with the sickle of contemplation.

Where was it that the disciples received the Spirit, the Paraclete? As they roamed the streets or as they sat by themselves on Mount Sion? As they busied themselves about idle matters, which were no concern of theirs, or as they gave themselves up wholeheartedly to prayer?[1]

This passage certainly expresses the dilemma in which one man at least found himself. But the condemnatory tone of much of the epistle, with its upbraiding of the brothers in such terms as the following, did little to smooth the path of transition and was ultimately counterproductive, arousing more passions than it soothed.

But in the city, the elements teem with such corruption that you too are contaminated and direly infected. Worldly vanity, meretriciously bedecked, keeps the interior man in bondage as surely as in prison, and does not suffer him to rise to heavenly thoughts.

For melodious birdsong, you hear men and women brawling, as well as their animals, mostly dogs and pigs, and an unspeakable din rings in your ears persistently. For green grass and leafy branches you have muddy streets to tramp each day. For the scent of flowers your nostrils drink in pestilential draughts of the intolerable stench of depravity.

All the alluring vanities of the city conspire to drown you in a cesspool of vices, for whoever sets out to preach pleasure, be his teaching never so deceptive, will make converts.[2]

A gentler tone would have been more effective, but Nicholas was determined to make his point. Possibly the friars were relieved when he resigned his office in protest and went off to live in seclusion.

Nicholas was in fact rather a lone voice. Most Carmelites did not see the changes made in the Rule as destroying the Order's spirit; rather, they saw the Order surviving because it knew how to read the signs of the times. As late as 1287 the General Chapter was able to testify 'We have left the world to be able to serve God in the castle of contemplation'. To the medieval Christian all religious were seen as contemplatives, there were not the distinctions abroad that plagued the church after the Council of Trent, contrasting the active life with that of the contemplative, with the implicit overtones of one vocation being 'more perfect' than another. If anything, Thomas Aquinas' teaching that 'sharing the fruits of contemplation' was to be preferred to a wholly retired life, would have been a sure indication that the former hermit brothers, even on Carmel itself, were not mistaken in making themselves available where there was need.

Within fifty years, then, the Order had changed definitively from being a purely eremitical group, to a mendicant Order with a contemplative-eremitical bias. Sustaining and balancing these tensions would be the task of all Carmelites throughout the Order's long history.

At this point it might be pertinent to insert a note on the garb of the friars, which at first distinguished them so clearly from their contemporaries.

It seems that the hermits on Carmel wore a habit of undyed wool, consisting of a plain tunic with a scapular over it. The scapular, part of most religious habits, was originally an apron that fell in two straight pieces front and back and protected the habit proper during work. A hood attached to the scapular and a leather belt completed the ensemble. A mantle, or 'carpeta', resembling a poncho and woven of alternating stripes of black or grey and white, was donned for ceremonial occasions and possibly doubled as a blanket at night.

The striped 'carpeta' of the Carmelites identified them as being of Eastern provenance and was in all likelihood borrowed from the Moslem milieu in which they originated. With time the garment came to symbolise for them the mantle Elijah bestowed on Elisha, the stripes being formed by scorch marks as it fell from the fiery chariot!

While perfectly acceptable in the East, the 'carpeta' proved to be an object of ridicule in the West. The poncho style was unusual for religious and it was difficult and expensive to obtain striped material woven in one piece. It seems that aspirants to the Order were put off entering if it meant that they were to be dressed 'like harlequins' and referred to as 'the stripey friars'. The appellation of Rue des Barres in Paris (street of the 'Stripies') dates from this period when a Carmelite house was founded in the vicinity.

Despite the efforts of some to retain the 'carpeta' as the distinctive garment of the Order, it was proven impractical and in 1287 was replaced everywhere by a white mantle. The 'stripey friars' became the 'white-friars' and the latter name has endured to this day.

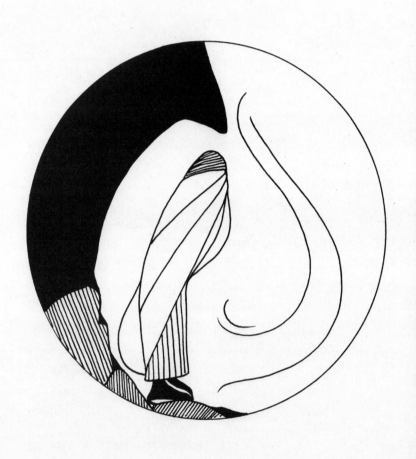

CHAPTER FIVE

THE SPIRIT OF ELIJAH

We have seen how the distinctive striped 'carpeta' of the Carmelites was associated with the mantle of Elijah, and when its colour and form changed it did not wholly lose this symbolism. In becoming the white cloak of Mary's purity and all-enveloping love it retained its significance also as preserving the memory of the prophet's gift of his cloak to Elisha, for Carmel's spirituality bridges the divide not only between East and West but between the Old Testament and the New.

As a prophet, Elijah epitomises the prophetic tradition of Israel. He challenges the Carmelite to be cast in the same prophetic mould of prayer, action and the proclamation of God's word.

Many things could be said about prophecy in the Bible and it would be impossible to touch on them all, but it is important to realise that much of what the prophets say is historically conditioned. The prophets were called to listen to God and read the signs of the times, reflecting with their whole being upon the Lord and his dealings with humanity. Thus they discerned in the life and experience of the Jewish people the presence of the One who had redeemed them from slavery and chosen them as his own, ratifying that choice by a Covenant destined to continue through all vicissitudes and infidelity on Israel's part.

Many Christians fail to understand that the Old Testament is relevant in its own right: for its teaching, its poetry, its wisdom, and for the insights it offers into the nature of creation and the role of society. Above all, it contains the patterns of thought and behaviour that fashioned Israel as a people. In this it provided the religious and cultural background of the formative years of Jesus, for neither he nor ourselves can be understood in a vacuum.

The prophetic teaching, as it matured, was brought to fulfilment in Jesus, Son of God and Son of Mary; but it also stands alone as a testimony to God's involvement in his people's history and self-understanding. Jesus' message, while being uniquely his, is not divorced from its origins in Law and prophecy. Jesus was dependent on the prophets, at least in part, for understanding his own Messianic vocation; and his daily life was directed by the Law, written and oral. Jesus brought both to full flowering, for his roots were deeply entwined with his people and their past.

Likewise in Christianity and the life of an Order, the teaching of forebears is always communicated within a certain tradition. But for this tradition to become a living reality it has to be made our own in our own way. It has to be creatively integrated by each one of us with our particular life experience and spiritual insights.

If we only take what is 'given' and mouth other people's answers we are 'second hand' persons. If, on the other hand, we do not attend to the wisdom of the past we lose our sense of 'rootedness' and connection. Each person is not a totally new beginning. We belong to one another in myriad ways and must learn from our spiritual heritage, family background, and all the influences that combine to make us what we are.

Jesus is the truest and greatest of prophets, the totally attentive one, the speaker for God *par excellence* and the interpreter of his works:

> The Lord has given me the tongue of a teacher, that I may know how to sustain the weary with a word. Morning by morning he wakens – wakens my ear – to listen as those who are taught.
>
> (Is. 50:4)

Just as the prophet does not transcend the Law but expounds its real meaning, does not make morality but reveals what is present, so Jesus does not come to destroy but to fulfil. He shows what the Law demands in total self-giving, not outward obligation alone:

> You have heard that it was said, 'An eye for an eye and a tooth for a tooth'. But I say to you, do not resist an evildoer. But if anyone strikes you on the right cheek, turn the other also; and if anyone wants to sue you and take your coat, give your cloak as well. Be perfect, therefore, as your heavenly Father is perfect.
>
> (Matt. 5:38–40, 48)

Jesus sees his teaching as fulfilling and perfecting the past. Everything he says or does is the truest and best of God's revelation in the Old Testament, enfleshed not in poetry or oracle but in a perfect human life.

By understanding the prophets we understand more of what Jesus summed up in himself, and the great prophets have power to speak to us now, just as they did to him. God's word is ever alive and active.

Jesus is not primarily the fulfilment of the Greek ideal of beauty and truth, nor of the Roman passion for precision and order. Jesus is the fulfilment of the Law and the prophets, himself embodying the prophetic vocation in all its fulness. He is transparent to God, fearless in proclaiming the truth, astute in reading the signs of the times, his life totally penetrated by and subjected to the Father in a response of love and humility.

Going back to the beginnings of prophecy as recorded in the Old Testament it is well to note that what we Christians term 'Historical Books' viz. Judges, I & II Samuel, I & II Kings, were termed 'early prophets' by the Jews, and this is how Jesus would have known them.

In Israel, history was not considered a mere chronicle of external events. The historical books contain a testimony of faith in the meaning of history as God's progressive revelation of himself within time. They are actually dominated by prophetic figures who perpetuate the tradition of Moses as spiritual leader. The Books of the Kings, for example, are less concerned with the rulers of Israel than with the prophets they heeded or rejected. Ahab was not a very important king *per se* compared with Omri, the builder of Samaria (I Kings 16:23–24); but Omri is passed over quickly in a few sentences, whereas Ahab and Jezebel are allocated disproportionate space because of their interaction with Elijah.

The real age of the prophets begins with Samuel, when we find a personal involvement in the message proclaimed and the task of proclaiming it. Samuel is not a 'professional prophet', one for whom prophecy is a career in which one can be trained. He is set apart from birth by God and called by name, being given a special mission.

It is Samuel who directs history in that he anoints Saul and David, indicating that the prophet is independent of and superior to the king. He, and those who succeed him, are keepers of Israel's conscience, challenging Israel's priests and rulers lest they sink into complacency and a settled, self-satisfied lifestyle.

The early prophets seem to have originated with a special class of 'holy men' with psychic or ecstatic powers which could be cultivated through certain techniques. This is a phenomena common to nearly all faiths. It involves a natural gift honed with practise and best activated within a group context (*cf.* I Sam. 19:20–21). Such would have been the 'sons of the prophets' who followed Elijah and Elisha. The drawback is that these 'natural' prophets could discern falsely or could be used by the establishment for political purposes, whereas the true prophet is able to stand alone if necessary. Ecstaticism as such is not repudiated but must be subservient to the inspiration of God. When Jeremiah confronts the prophet Hananiah he speaks as one who has truly listened, not one who is proclaiming what others want to hear (Jer. 28:1–17).

It is very probable that the prophetic books, and stories about the prophets, were transmitted by disciples who were considered sharers in the same prophetic charism in a lesser way; just as members of religious Orders are said to participate in the founder's charism to some degree.

✆

In Elijah we have the epitome of the Old Testament prophet. He appeared with Moses at the Transfiguration and was expected to precede the Messiah.

Yet Elijah is not the greatest of the prophets when compared with someone like Jeremiah or Isaiah. Elijah seems to have been chosen as the prophetic archetype because he is like the ancient 'holy man' of the desert, wild and free, yet he is also a man consumed by a sense of personal mission like the classical writing prophets.

Zeal is the keynote of the Elijah cycle. In him there are no half-measures, whether he is rebuking the king, challenging false prophets or railing against injustice. He is leader of a group yet towers above it.

When Elijah first appears in the Book of Kings he seems to have been a professional prophet for some time. He springs from nowhere, no account is given of a special call; but he is the one who stands before the living God and hears his voice – a voice with a message for himself and others.

From their place of origin, Mount Carmel, sacred to Elijah's memory, and from their cells, erected 'beside the spring', the first Latin hermits cherished an obvious spiritual affinity, through their location, with this great figure from the past. Elijah was the hermits' inspiration. They thought of him as being present to them in a special way, as one who pre-eminently combined prayer and action in an integrated whole.

The hermits drank from the source which had presumably supplied Elijah with life-giving water; their mode of dress was such as to recall his own attire – mantle and leather belt. Thus they considered themselves as incorporated into the company of those who revered Elijah and Elisha and participated in their spirit; a 'community' of prophets, not just notable individuals.

But it is one thing to venerate a person who embodies a vocation and feel a deep indentification with his story, shared and pondered upon. It is quite another thing to claim *actual linear descent* through the 'sons of the prophet' and their reputed leader.

In fact, even before the Carmelites came on the scene, many in the early church claimed that the whole monastic tradition could be traced back to Elijah himself. With time, the attribution to Elijah of being the first monk ceased to be a hypothesis in the minds of his devotees and became an established fact of history. Elijah the first monk lived on Mount Carmel with a monastic community of disciples. In the fifth century Cassian writes of the monastery Elijah founded on Mount Carmel, 'illustrious for the virtue and reputation of the one who had lived there'. Already Carmel was being revered as the place of Elijah's domicile, though there is no evidence to support this. Elijah seems to have been a wandering prophet, not stable in one place like a true monk. He was far more the roving preacher, the 'mendicant', than the settled cenobite.

The Christian cult of Elijah was probably introduced on the mountain by Byzantine monks in the sixth century to counteract the cult of the pagan god Helios. By erecting a monastery on the promontory and another at the cave of Elijah they chose sites directly in opposition to Jewish traditional shrines on the east side of the mountain. This of course does not negate their importance, for Elijah is not bound to any one place or time; he transcends both.

The Latin hermits, established on the former Byzantine site in the Wadi es Siah, inherited and cherished the Elijan tradition. Here they had their identity. Here they had taken root in an alien land and made it their own.

But on coming to Europe the Carmelites left the place that was sacred to them and their physical closeness to the prophetic cult. In new lands they found it difficult to be accepted on equal terms with the Franciscans and Dominicans who had such charismatic founders. Who could *they* point to? Nothing seemed to be known of B. though he was speedily assigned the name of Brocard. Surely Elijah was the one who was their true precursor.

The Carmelite Constitutions of 1281, our only extant link with early legislation apart from the Rule, gives the following account of the Order's origin in the Prologue:

> *To give a reply to those who ask how our Order began and why we are called Brothers of Our Lady of Mount Carmel, this is what you must say: We declare, bearing witness to the truth, that from the time when the prophets Elijah and Elisha dwelt devoutly on Mount Carmel, the holy fathers both of the Old and New Testament, whom the contemplation of holy things drew to the solitude of the same mountain, have without doubt led praiseworthy lives there, by the fountain of Elijah, in holy penitence, which they have maintained faithfully and successively.*
>
> *Their successors, after the Incarnation of Christ, built an oratory there in honour of the Blessed Virgin Mary, and took her for their patron. Later on, by privilege of the Holy See, they called themselves Brothers of Our Lady of Mount Carmel.*[1]

Many Carmelites clung to this literal tradition right into the mid-twentieth century, though the claim was hotly disputed by others even in the Middle Ages.

The very fact of being associated with the place hallowed by Elijah was seen as sufficient justification for the early Carmelites to claim direct descent from him and the 'sons of the prophets'; but there were also a number of lacunae in the story of how the Order had continued and developed in unbroken line from Old Testament times to the present. Hence the medieval friars set about filling in the gaps rather than attending to their actual history as it was lived in the friaries of Europe.

John Baconthorpe, a Norfolk Carmelite educated by the friars of Blakeney in the early 1300s wrote that the Order could be traced back to Samuel who was the first to institute a prophetic school. One such group, whose office was to contemplate God, settled on Mount Carmel and, on coming in contact with Elijah, became his disciples.

Others said that John the Baptist lived with the same community in his youth. They accepted his teaching, transferring their allegiance to Christ when on pilgrimage to Jerusalem, where they were present at the outpouring of the Spirit on the day of Pentecost. New figures were incorporated into the Order's hagiography, including a fictitious John, Patriarch of Jerusalem, reputed writer of the first Carmelite Rule. Other people and events of similar fictitious provenance were not lacking as the Order gained recruits and ever greater confidence in its literary inventiveness.

However, while these far-fetched biographies are just that – far-fetched and totally fictitious, the kernel of teaching contained in them is valid. One of the most formative texts used by medieval Carmelites was a book entitled *The Institution of the First Monks*. Whether this originated with the Carmelites or not, it was certainly popularised among them in the fourteenth century by Philip Ribot, a Spaniard. In it Elijah is lauded as founding

figure of monks and model of Carmelites. The
following extract is a fine example:

*The word of the Lord came to Elijah saying: 'Depart
from here and go Eastwards and hide yourself by the
brook Cherith, that is over against the Jordan, and there
you shall drink from the brook and I have commanded
the ravens to feed you'.*

*Now these salutary commands, which the Holy Spirit
prompted Elijah to obey, and this promise of things desir-
able which were set before him as a goal for his aspirations,
should be weighed word for word with the greatest care by
us, monks and solitaries, not in a merely historical but
rather in a mystical sense, for they contain the fulness of
our vocation; that is, they point the way to prophetic
perfection, the goal of the religious eremitical life.*

*In regard to that life, we may distinguish two aims,
the one of which we may attain to, with the help of God's
grace and our own efforts and virtuous living. This is to
offer God a heart holy and pure from all actual stain of
sin. This aim we achieve when we become perfect and
hidden in Cherith – that is, in charity, of which the wise
man says: Love covers all offences. It was to bring Elijah
to this state that God said to him: Hide yourself by the
brook Cherith.*

*The other aim of this life is something that can be
bestowed upon us only by God's bounty; namely to taste
in our hearts and experience in our minds, not only after
death but even during this mortal life, something of the
power of the divine presence and the bliss of heavenly
glory. And this is to drink from the brook of the enjoy-
ment of God, which is the reward God promised Elijah
when he said: There you shall drink from the brook.*[2]

Taken all in all, the Carmelites of the Middle Ages
and beyond were guided in their self-understanding

by a mixture of legend, history, mystical exhortation and no small amount of comedy. But the fact remains that for the Order Elijah was and is the pre-eminent model and embodiment of the Carmelite vocation. He is Carmel's by tradition, myth and unbroken veneration since the Latin hermits settled in the wadi. His story shapes the Order's spirituality and nourishes its devotion. So strong are the symbols of the Elijah stories that they appeal perennially to the subconscious under the forms of water, fire, wilderness, the cleft rock, the gentle breeze; while the prophet's cry 'With zeal I have been zealous for the Lord the God of Hosts' has become the Order's motto emblazoned on its crest.

Looking at the story of Elijah as handed down to posterity in the Book of the Kings, three aspects of his personality strike the reader: he is a man of the people, a man of action and a man of prayer.

As a man of the people Elijah is intimately involved with the community as a whole and with the individuals who form it. He relates with the widow of Zarephath as a person in need and confidently draws out her generosity of response (I Kings 17: 8–24). The widow has only a handful of meal in a jar and a little oil in a jug but at Elijah's encouragement she can share it so that it multiplies to feed her household, just as Jesus shared a few loaves and fishes with a great multitude.

Elijah, filled as he is with the Spirit (or Breath) of the Lord communicates this Breath to the widow's son and he lives.

Elijah is the one who enters into relationships, into the give and take of life without fear, because he knows himself to be standing always in the Lord's presence (*cf.* I Kings 17:1).

As a man of the people Elijah confronts injustice

when Ahab appropriates Naboth's vineyard (I Kings 12:1–29). He speaks in God's name, defending the rights of the poor to their land, to their identification with their familial heritage. What is God's gift is not to be taken away by the powerful at their whim and fancy. To speak for the powerless and, by doing so, confront the oppressor, is part of the prophetic calling, and it can be done in small ways as well as big. To do nothing in the face of injustice can be as 'irreligious' as actually perpetrating the wrong. Far from being meek and retiring, the Carmelite is one who is compelled to speak out when necessary, regardless of what might be prudent and safe.

As a man of action, Elijah challenges the priests of Baal on Mount Carmel, calling on them in a radical way to prove their god's existence, forcing the people to decide for or against the God of Israel:

> How long with you go limping with two different opinions? If the Lord is God, follow him: but if Baal, then follow him. The people did not answer a word.
>
> (I Kings 18:21)

Martin Buber interprets this 'limping' using the image of a bird who, hopping along a branch, comes to an intersection where the branch forks into two twigs. If the bird continues to keep a foot on each twig and tries to move forward like that it will slip through the centre space into a void. It must decide one way or another if it wants to survive. The prophet, therefore, is one who, by word and work, causes others to question where they stand, what decisions they should make. To hesitate too long or to try and take two paths at the same time means annihilation. Over-cautiousness stifles life.

It is only when Elijah (etymology: my God is Yahweh) has confounded the priests of Baal that rain comes to refresh the parched earth, heralded by a little cloud rising out of the sea as he prays on the mountain.

As a man of prayer we see Elijah totally dependent on God's providence at the brook Cherith (I Kings 17:3–7). He is one who listens in solitude, knowing when to remain in retirement and when to approach others. All his actions spring from attending to God's voice, God's directives.

So it is that from Mount Carmel with all its activity Elijah proceeds to the desert and to Horeb. Far from feeling elated about his triumph over the priests of Baal he is exhausted as if, like Jesus, power has gone out of him and he realises his emptiness and need. And once again the Lord approaches through intermediaries as at Cherith to provide food for the journey (I Kings 19:4–8).

Elijah is one who shows courage in active trust, therefore he continues in dark faith, even when he feels depressed and rejected.

It is at Horeb that Elijah receives what might be deemed his deeply personal call when he attains to Mosaic stature. Like Moses at Horeb (Ex. 19:20), hidden in the rock (Ex. 33:22) he experiences the presence of God in the gentle breeze which symbolises the intimacy of revelation communicated to the solitary soul.

Hermits have always loved hidden places; the surroundings of nature, the wind, the rain, the sun, which facilitate exposure to silent and attentive listening far from human distraction. As God inspired Moses 'mouth to mouth' with the Spirit, who is called the 'kiss' between Father and Son, so on Horeb Elijah realises that God's Spirit is breathing into him and offering new life, new birth, a new sense of mission.

Only now does Elijah understand that God's nearness is not found in noise and outward victory but in
the depths of the silent heart. He rises then with
courage, ready to start afresh, find a successor to
share the prophetic gift with, and enter once more
into the arena of political and social involvement.

The Order of Carmel, in contemplating Elijah, sees
in him a great leader and listener, wholly attentive to
God, zealous in God's service, realistically involved
with people. But it is one thing to put on Elijah's
mantle and be one of his spiritual descendants. It is
another to really encounter God in solitude in a
deeply personal way, which is the whole reason
behind the journey the Carmelite makes into the
desert.

There is no room for complacency. A prophet, and
all Christians are called to be such, has to be continually attentive, marginal, non-dependent on worldly
values, even if feeling despondent like Elijah, and 'the
only one left'.

In Elijah, as in Jesus, solitude and apostolate are
linked. There is a listening to the Father in silence
which then overflows into involvement in the
marketplace. Everyone needs both prayer and action
for a truly integrated personality. Even such a great
contemplative as Teresa of Avila stresses in her writings that there is an active element in the eremitical
life. Works of love, the pouring out of self in the
service of the community, are incumbent on all.
Works in fact assume an even greater importance the
more one journeys into God, otherwise there is a
danger that prayer becomes mere self-absorbtion.
Prayer is proved by works, not fine feelings. In the
highest realms of the spiritual life there is no repose.
The one who prays is fired with Elijah's zeal to estab-

lish the reign of God and thus thinks of nothing but
how to further God's cause, not his/her own peaceful
existence.

In Jewish tradition, because Elijah was taken up to
God while still alive, he lives now to intercede for the
people. To intercede is the Carmelite's primary role –
to intercede with the whole of one's being. That
means being in touch with God but also in touch with
one's humanity, with the humanity of others, and
with the needs of the poor. It means thirsting for solitude and prayer while having the courage to
proclaim God's word. It means inspiring others to
share in the mission entrusted to all who seek the
Lord with a sincere heart.

The prayer for the feast of Elijah, celebrated by
Carmelites each year on July 20th, encapsulates all
that he means for the Order as father and friend.

> Almighty, everliving God,
> your prophet Elijah, our father,
> lived always in your presence
> and was zealous for the honour due to your name.
> May we, your servants, always seek your face
> and bear witness to your love.
> Through Christ our Lord. Amen.

CHAPTER SIX

MARY – LADY OF THE PLACE

While Elijah has stood for the active element in the Carmelite vocation, Mary has been present from the first as the hidden feminine principle. Carmel is known as Mary's Order, *totus Marianus*. The first oratory in the Wadi es Siah was dedicated to her and the hermits were known as the Brothers of the Blessed Mary of Mount Carmel. The earliest extant profession formula promised obedience to 'God and to blessed Mary'. She was with the brothers in their solitude; the woman to whom they looked as 'lady of the place'.

As the first Carmelites came from a feudal society they transposed their devotion into the feudal spirituality with which they were familiar. They lived 'in allegiance to Christ', the liege Lord to whom they owed undivided homage. But every lord has a lady, and who but Mary was Christ's 'lady' and thus *their* lady in a special way. Christ as Lord held in fief the hermitages in the wadi, but there was another unseen presence whose beauty was reflected in the very land the brothers occupied.

This was the era when the human rather than the divine Christ was foremost in people's consciousness.

Mount Carmel was situated in the very country of Jesus. There he had lived, like us in all things but sin. His mother was a human mother, a sister and friend to her contemporaries, a woman among women. Writing of the iconography of the thirteenth century, Henri Focillon says that it was evangelic and natural, mother and son being tenderly united in painting and sculpture:

> The thirteenth century surrounded the youthful image of the virgin with an affectionate fervour which, while glorifying woman, respected her femininity, just as, in the beauty of the angels, it preserved, as a fadeless flower, the fleeting charms of adolescence among the children of men. From Annunciation to Coronation she retains her birthright of grace, derived from her human clay. She is no longer the stone idol of earlier ages, but the celestial sister of human mothers.[1]

In this period too, Elizabeth of Hungary and Louis of Thuringia embodied the ideal marriage. Louis as lord allowed his beloved Elizabeth full freedom of his lands, his possessions, his revenues, so that she could pour herself out generously for the sick and needy. She was no longer a cipher of her husband but a person in her own right. The tender terms they used to address one another, 'dear brother', 'dear sister', revealed their mutual love and devotion. Even so the early Carmelites saw Mary as their 'sister', with full permission to administer their lands, and indeed everything that was theirs.

Mary brings to Carmel a gentle, loving presence. Carmel is hers; there she holds sway as 'lady', just as the crusader prince, Louis, allowed his lady Elizabeth full freedom of personal expression in giving loving service to those dependent on her.

As sister, as mother, Mary enshrines the primal human symbol of mother and child. Religious or not, everyone can respond to this icon which touches our most basic human instincts. We are all the fruit of a mother's womb whether we are kings or paupers, as Solomon writes so movingly:

> I also am mortal, like everyone else,
> a descendant of the first-formed child of earth;
> and in the womb of my mother I was molded into
>   flesh,
> within the period of ten months compacted into
>   blood,
> from the seed of man and the pleasure of
>   marriage.
> And when I was born, I began to breathe the
>   common air,
> and fell upon the kindred earth;
> my first sound was a cry, as is true of all.
> I was nursed with care in swaddling clothes,
> for no king has had a different beginning of
>   existence;
> there is for all one entrance into life and one way
>   out.
>
> (Wis. 7:1–6)

In bringing Carmel to Europe it was as if a piece of the holy mountain was established in the friaries of the West. Every Carmel was Mary's – her domain, her house. There she was mother to her children. There she welcomed all who approached the brothers; her hands, her eyes, her heart working through their service and their care. She was a presence to them in their solitude and in their apostolate.

But Mary is not only the lady of the place. She *is* the

land of Carmel. The attribution of earth, land, as feminine is deeply embedded in the human psyche. Woman is earthiness, mystery, unexplored depths. Likewise, Israel as land is feminine. She is God's country called to a relationship of bridal response with the Lord. God leads Israel into the wilderness to espouse her in righteousness and justice, in steadfast love and mercy (Hos. 2:9), and later he changes her desert into a garden of rejoicing:

> For the Lord will comfort Zion;
> he will comfort all her waste places
> and will make her wilderness like Eden,
> her desert like the garden of the Lord;
> joy and gladness will be found in her,
> thanksgiving and the voice of song.
>
> (Is. 51:3)

With this biblical imagery in the background it is understandable why the early Carmelites liked to ponder on Elijah's vision of the little cloud rising from the sea as he prayed on Carmel, seeing in it a prefigurement of Mary. In the antiphon *Flos Carmeli* Mary is called the 'blossoming vine' because many blossoms herald a rich harvest of grapes. In the same way, a cloud heralds the advent of rain which will water the earth and make it fertile.

In the Middle Ages clouds were believed to be water-carrying vessels. Thus Mary, as Christ-bearer, was the one carrying the water of life. She brings healing and refreshment to the parched earth, just as she is also the earth which receives the rain. There is in Mary that rhythmn of giving and receiving, of fulness and emptiness, which makes her so truly woman. In pouring herself out she receives life anew. Bowed down in prayer like Elijah, the Carmelite waits for the sign of Mary's presence in hope and perseverance, knowing that she brings her Son with her, for mother and child are inseparable. The Son, as rain, penetrates the ground of Carmel so that the Order may mirror Mary's fruitfulness, beauty and responsiveness. Mary is the woman of the Eucharistic bread, for she is mother of the Word which accomplishes all it has been sent out to do. As she herself is fed by the Word, she can draw others to the Food that lasts forever:

> For my thoughts are not your thoughts,
> nor are your ways my ways says the Lord.
> For as the heavens are higher than the earth
> so are my ways higher than your ways
> and my thoughts than your thoughts.
> For as the rain and the snow come down from
>   heaven,
> and do not return there until they have watered
>   the earth,
> making it bring forth and sprout,
> giving seed to the sower and bread to the eater,
> so shall my word be that goes out from my mouth;
> it shall not return to me empty,
> but it shall accomplish that which I purpose
> and succeed in the thing for which I sent it.
> For you shall go out in joy
> and be led back in peace;
> and the mountains and hills before you
> shall burst into song,
> and all the trees of the field shall clap their hands.
> Instead of the thorn shall come up the cypress;
> instead of the briar shall come up the myrtle;
> and it shall be to the Lord for a memorial,
> for an everlasting sign that shall not be cut off.
>
> (Is. 55:8–13)

The first Carmelites, who by the Rule of St Albert were required to celebrate daily Mass, would have received in Communion the bread and wine made from the wheat and grapes grown in the very soil of the Holy Land, symbol of both Israel and Mary. The 'firstfruits' of the Carmelite Order were thus linked with the mother of God in their central act of worship and praise.

Mary is in a sense herself the 'firstfruits' of Carmel, a special gift to the Order dedicated to her. But what does the bible mean by 'firstfruits' and what is their significance?

For the Israelites, the produce of the Promised Land was symbolic of the totality of the Lord's goodness towards his people. It was manifested in the loving providence with which he had guided them through the desert and settled them in their own country.

They ploughed and sowed and watered the sacred soil, but only God could give the increase. Therefore the year was punctuated with little 'harvest festivals' as each crop was gathered in and the Lord thanked for it.

Together with other Middle Eastern countries the Jews developed the custom of offering back to God the first of every crop. The newest, tenderest and best part belonged to him and was 'given back' as it were in the context of a sacred ceremony, blending gratitude for Israel's history, the donor's personal history, and God's goodness (*cf.* Deut. 26:1–11).

The Israelites were to return to God the produce of the land of promise, and they did this by offering the 'firstfruits', for the first signified the whole harvest. In offering the first of any crop all that followed was considered sanctified and could be partaken of in the spirit of thanksgiving.

Christ, as first to rise from the dead, is likened to those 'firstfuits'. He is the first and the best of humankind, offered to the Father as a pure sacrifice. But he rises not for himself alone. He rises as one of the human race, one of ourselves. He guarantees that we, the rest of the harvest, will one day be with him in glory.

Mary has attained that joy already. She is now where her Son is and where we too will be one day. Our Easter will follow that of Jesus, as did hers.

Mary, in her surrender, her purity, her holiness, is the first offering after Christ, and she wants to bring us with her to a similar way of being. She is the 'first Carmelite' and in her the rest are Marian, each in his or her own way.

The perfection of the firstfruits lies not in their sameness but in their variety. The thank-offering made to God for the harvest is not just comprised of shiny red apples, succulent grapes and plump figs. There is the onion, the leek, the cucumber in their solid plainness. There are not only the golden grains of wheat and barley, but the insignificant parsley, garlic and dill which add flavour and make insipid food palatable. So Carmel is a land that, to be a true image of what God wants it to be, must be a micro-cosm of the whole Church, bringing forth fruits in a variety of people. The soil of Carmel should nourish the seeds that form a people and community out of many different races, backgrounds and personalities, each adding to the richness and variety of the whole.

Mary has been the best and most productive of soils. She is the woman spoken of by the psalmist as a fruitful vine in the heart of the house, her children as olive shoots around her table (Ps. 128:3).

When Jesus told the parable of the sower and the seed (Matt. 21:1–23) he likened each person to a different ground that received the word according to its capacity. Mary is the good ground which brought forth a hundredfold, and she encourages us to be like her, utilising whatever is our own life's soil to the full. She brings the gentle rain that fructifies what is barren in us, and she does this for *all*. She does not discriminate between righteous and unrighteous, just and unjust. Like a true mother she loves each child without attending to whether or not they are 'worthy' of love. In this she reflects the perfection of God (Matt. 6:45).

Mary is not some esoteric being, she is a woman of the land, a woman of Israel. One who has lived there writes as follows:

> I am led to tell you that what my sojourn in this land has changed as much as anything else is my image of Mary. In previous years that could hardly be any other than what I have received through Piero della Francesca's paintings or Gerard Manley Hopkins' poems or Gounod's music – the image of some dreamy ethereal young lady untouched by everyday toil.
>
> But since that time I have met the peasant women of Galilee. So now the image that comes spontaneously to mind is of a woman with strong hands, sinewy through much work; and of a face whose skin is rough from exposure to the sun and the wind; of feet that are broad spread through climbing the hills around Narareth bare foot; but above all, of eyes that are steady, and a mouth that is firm through enduring the sorrows of the refugee, the poor and the oppressed.[2]

Mary leads us to Jesus as a real woman who has known poverty and toil, not as a woman who has had a quiet, prayer-wrapped existence divorced from the nitty-gritty of daily life, with its pain and suffering as well as its joy.

As mother of Carmel, devotion to Mary was a recognised aspect of Carmelite spirituality in the Middle Ages. In 1287 the General Chapter invoked her intercession as the one 'in whose service and honour our Order was founded'. From the fourteenth century onwards there was much literature produced linking Carmel with Mary and Elijah. It was said that, as Nazareth was only three miles from the holy mountain, the Virgin used to visit it often with the child Jesus. The Rule was supposed to embody the Virgin's way of life in every detail. The Carmelites regularly dedicated their churches to Mary under one of her main titles of the Immaculate Conception, the Annunciation or the Assumption. Aylesford, the most important English house, was founded under the patronage of the Assumption. The white mantle came to be seen as a symbol of Mary's purity and, with the Franciscans, the Carmelites championed the doctrine of the Immaculate Conception at the universities.

But the living of Carmel was always more important than theologising. In seeing the Rule of Carmel as a re-enactment of Mary's lifestyle, the Order was really claiming Mary as being identified with them as sister-companion, her life and theirs linked in numerous ways.

Mary is the embodiment of all we are called to be as Christians – not because she is different but because she is the same.

All that can be said of Mary can be said of us. She is the most perfect Christian, the truest disciple of Jesus. All her sanctity comes from her likeness to Christ, as does ours, from the first moment of conception until the culmination of her personal history in the glorious Assumption.

What the great Marian dogmas say in their essence is that Mary embodies the life of grace. She does not have to earn anything, she has only to receive, placing no obstacle in the way of the inflowing gifts of God.

The greatest gift we have all received is the gift of life, something quite unearned. If we think about it we had no say in our conception, in who our parents were, what kind of home and upbringing and education we had. Our genetic inheritance was not chosen by ourselves. All that was given was given without our choice and without our permission.

It is fascinating to read about the human embryo and how everything about us is potentially in existence while we are still in the womb: our eye colour, our physical features, our brain, our I.Q., even every hair follicle is programmed in. And like Mary, we too were conceived with all the gifts and potential God wished us to have for the fulfilment of our own unique vocation.

Mary was gifted and destined for a particular role in salvation history, that of being God's mother. But she was not a different kind of person from ourselves. The only difference is that she never chose to sin, never chose against the person God meant her to be. And that too was gift and grace, not something earned.

Like us, Mary was born into a sinful world. She too had to make difficult choices. She could make mistakes. She had her own share of annoying mannerisms, no doubt: she burned the dinner, or laughed too loudly or forgot to tidy up. She is not woman in the abstract, an amalgam of bland 'perfection'. She is a particular woman with her own particular physical, psychical and spiritual make up. How fascinating if the veil could be drawn back for us to see her about her daily tasks. Most likely we could not pick her out from a crowd unless she was our special friend, recognised by her walk or the toss of her head.

The details of Mary's life are hidden in obscurity. All we know of her can be gleaned from the Gospels where she is shown primarily as a woman of faith; a faith sustained by a life of choosing – choosing the will of God, day in, day out.

Mary never sullied the gift of life entrusted to her, the unique vocation God had in mind for her. Mary never chose against love, and love is unmerited, it is the greatest mystery of all.

We know that when we experience love in our life it is always pure gift. Oscar Wilde says that 'Love is a sacrament to be received only on our knees with the words "Lord, I am not worthy".' We are *not* worthy – and yet we love and are loved, and so touch God.

Grace is the love of God freely given to us from the first moment of our conception, moulding us into the pattern of Christ if we respond, forming us so that, as with Mary, he may become incarnate through our flesh and be given anew to the world.

With Mary we can paraphrase the opening words of the Epistle to the Ephesians and claim them as our own:

Blessed be the God and Father of our Lord Jesus Christ, who has blessed my life in Christ with every spiritual blessing. He chose me before the foundation of the world, that I should be holy and blameless before him. He destined me in love to be his child through Jesus Christ, and I have been destined and appointed to live for the praise of his glory.

(cf. Eph. 1:3–5)

This is what the Assumption is saying: that we too,

like Mary, body and soul, are chosen and called to live for the praise of God's glory in the thousand and one seemingly insignificant choices of every day which shape us for eternity.

In Mary's Assumption we see her 'glory' – her whole life made radiant, every aspect of her person penetrated by the Godhead, spirit and flesh. This life of an ordinary Galilean peasant woman is rendered eternally fruitful and glorious. 'The Almighty has done great things for me, holy is *his* name'.

At the end of our life, the light of God will reveal who we are and have become. What we *are* will then shine through, not the image we have tried to project. Plainly and simply what we really are will be revealed and our disguises and untruths will drop away.

This can sound frightening, for we are usually so busy shielding ourselves from total exposure, but in eternity we shall find it a joy to be seen, loved and accepted just as we are.

Meanwhile our work on earth is to glorify the Father as Jesus did by finishing the work he gives us to do; work done in darkness now, but with deep faith that exile ends in glory. Then we shall see all things in their true perspective.

St Thérèse, in one of her letters to Celine, encourages her with the thought that even now God sees us in glory, sees us as we are ultimately meant to be and are called to be. How then is it possible to get bogged down in meanness and pettiness. One day we too will experience our personal Easter.

Jesus has already become, as Paul says 'the first-fruits from the dead' and Mary is the first to follow him. She *is* us and holds us in her surrender. The Carmelite knows this instinctively.

෴

While the great Marian feasts of the Church were the focus of Carmelite devotion to Mary in the Middle Ages, there was growing up, quietly and imperceptibly, another feast – that of our Lady of Mount Carmel. This feast has an unusual history, developing spontaneously as an expression of the Order's love for the Mother of God, and gaining widespread popularity through the scapular devotion.

It seems that a feast of Our Lady's Patronage was first introduced among Carmelites in England. In 1386 Nicholas of Lynn gives the Collect for a Mass of the Solemn Commemoration of the Blessed Virgin, a feast instituted 'to honour and thank the Blessed Virgin for the favours conferred on the Order, and especially for its Marian title'. The Collect runs thus:

O God,
who has adorned with the title of the most
    excellent Virgin
and your mother, Mary,
the humble Order consecrated to you,
and in whose defence you have worked miracles,
favourably grant that we may now experience the
    help
and afterwards participate in the eternal joys
of her whose memory we celebrate.[3]

This feast notwithstanding, most houses seem to have kept the Assumption as the principal Marian celebration, though the choice was not universal. Teresa of Avila mentions the 'feast of Our Lady in August' (the Assumption) several times, but never the feast of Our Lady of Carmel, even though she is most particular in dating her letters and foundations in reference to the liturgical year.

The Commemoration of Our Lady of Mount

Carmel, begun as a simple memorial in England, was prescribed to be kept solemnly in *all* houses of the Order in 1609 with a proper Mass, vigil and octave added. It was then extended to the universal church in 1726. The title chosen is symbolic of Mary, mistress and queen of contemplatives, as interpreted by the Carmelite spirit and Rule.

In the present Mass and Office there are two main symbols interlocking: that of the mountain and the garden. The mountain recalls the terrain of the first hermits' settlement; the garden because Carmel is not an arid mountain but one of lush verdure, a 'garden land'. In some ways these two symbols are contradictory, or rather, each complements the other in highlighting a certain paradox in the Carmelite vocation.

Mountains are symbols of stability, power, closeness to God. In the Bible mountains are places of meeting with the deity – Sinai (Horeb), Zion, Tabor, Hermon. One ascends to an altar, going up towards a transcendent God as a transcendent being oneself. The mountain speaks of solitude and the desert, for the higher one ascends the more barren and dangerous the land becomes. The mountain peak is generally inaccessible and it takes courage to proceed upwards rather than rest in the plain. Mountains have always offered adventurous people a challenge not to be ignored.

In the writings of St John of the Cross especially, Carmel is replete with this mountain imagery. The *Ascent of Mount Carmel* speaks of the way by which we go direct to the source and summit – God alone. Contemplation is a costly business demanding total dedication. In the present prayer for the feast of Our Lady of Carmel the mountain one ascends is Christ himself:

Lord God,
you willed that the Order of Carmel
should be named in honour of the Blessed Virgin
  Mary,
mother of your Son.
Through her prayers as we honour her today,
bring us to your holy Mountain, Christ our Lord
who lives and reigns with you and the Holy Spirit
one God for ever and ever. Amen.

Contemplation is to scale the heights with and in Christ, just as Jesus himself prayed in solitude on mountains. Like a mountain, Jesus has stability, He is rooted in the Father. He loves silent and solitary communion with the Father away from the noise of the world.

Our Lady's role is to bring us to the mountain which is Jesus in a manner accessible to and understandable by all. When we look at her we realise that we don't need physical strength so much as a disposition to give God all he asks. With her we must continue from the joy of acceptance at the Annunciation to the sorrow of Calvary and from there to the outpouring of the Spirit at Pentecost.

The garden imagery counteracts the bleakness of the mountain. Naturally speaking, Carmel is not a forbidding peak. It is in an area of great beauty, surrounded by water in a land where water is precious.

A garden locked is my sister, my bride,
a garden locked, a fountain sealed.
Your channel is an orchard of pomegranates
with all the choicest fruits,
henna with nard,
nard and saffron, calamus and cinnamon

with all the trees of frankincense,
myrrh and aloes with all chief spices–
a garden fountain, a well of living water
and flowing streams from Lebanon.
Awake, O north wind,
and come, O south wind!
Blow upon my garden
that its fragrance may be wafted abroad.
Let my beloved come into his garden
and eat its choicest fruits.

(Song 4:12–16)

The garden image is wholly Marian. The mountain has overtones of the masculine and is associated with Christ. Carmel as garden images Mary, most beautiful, most fruitful, because in the soil of her heart and body God himself was brought forth for the world.

Both Teresa of Avila and John of the Cross use the image of the garden as symbol of the individual soul – receptive to wind and water, seed and growth.

Carmel is the garden where we meet God and surrender to him in faith as Mary did, our fruitfulness coming from a continual pondering on the Word in silence and prayer. This is the hidden principle in the Church which is 'Marian' in the deepest sense; even the Carmelite habit of brown material reminds us of this earthiness.

Each person is a 'garden' for God, a 'place' waiting to be prepared:

Sow for yourselves righteousness;
reap steadfast love;
break up the fallow ground;
for it is time to seek the Lord,
that he may come and rain righteousness upon you.

(Hos. 10:12)

As Teresa of Avila would say, it is prayer that prepares the garden and causes it to fructify in God's good time. Our part is to live the 'liturgy of daily life', every moment a prayer; thus becoming 'garden' for God as Mary was. And in honouring her we honour her Son, for she is the woman who gave him life:

> Do not forget the pangs of your mother.
> Remember that through your parents you were
>   born;
> how can you repay what they have given you?
>
> (Sir. 7:27b–28)

Carmel is all Mary's, but only so that it can be totally given to Jesus by her and through her. It is her Order because it is primarily his; and all that the mother has is given for and to the Son in total surrender.

CHAPTER SEVEN

THE ADVENT OF THE NUNS

Every Order that has a long history goes through periods of decline and reform, periods when the ideals are almost forgotten and periods when the light of fervour burns strongly.

Carmel has been no exception to these alternating rhythms. The heart of Carmel is prayer and solitude because the Order originated with a group of hermits, but it has also had to integrate its solitary, prayerful side with community living and apostolic activity. This is bound to set up tensions, and indeed all religious life has to be continually re-assessed and re-examined even in the present day. The balance is delicate and needs regular adjustment.

On coming to Europe, members of the Order-in-embryo had had to discern where they fitted into the society they found. We have seen that they soon changed from being primarily an eremitical group and joined the ranks of the mendicants. The blending of Elijah and Mary, apostolate and prayer, in their evolving sense of who they were, generated a basic Carmelite spirituality that still had to be lived out on a daily basis and find practical expression by way of supportive structures. It meant that from the first the

Carmelites were adapting and experimenting, making it difficult to form new members. These expect to find a stable, tested way of life in which to be incorporated gradually and surely. It is not surprising therefore to find that Carmel needed time to find a *modus vivendi* that enshrined the charism of prayer while being alive to the needs and signs of the times.

As the Middle Ages progressed the Carmelites, together with other mendicant Orders, were in a spiritual decline. The privileges accorded them as academics had resulted in difficulties both outside and within the religious life. The three main problems were those related to poverty, observance of the common life and enclosure. Each area needed vigilance because the initial founding inspiration was always subject to the temptation to settle down to a spiritually mediocre existence.

Poverty proved to be a contentious issue from the first, since poverty was one of the bedrocks of the mendicant movement. As an ideal it was lauded. When it came to practical matters it was harder to assess. For the Franciscans especially, poverty became the cause of innumerable splits within the Order and Carmel was not untouched by the controversy.

As mendicants theoretically possessed no revenues or farmlands they had to rely on alms plus what they earned from their spiritual ministry, teaching etc. The friars often received bequests from the merchant class who were not wealthy enough to endow a monastic foundation but would appreciate burial and prayers within a friary. In this situation it was tempting to encourage legacies and fees by devious means, such as giving lenient penances to benefactors. Also, within many Carmelite communities the strict poverty of the Rule that 'no one may lay claim to anything as his own' was interpreted very loosely. Brothers began to acquire their own books and cells, thus making it harder for them to be moved around. Communities were divided into the 'haves' and 'have nots'. Reform movements within the Order (and Teresa of Avila was no exception to this) nearly always began with a return to the original emphasis on poverty as an equalising force, embracing everyone as regards a common standard of living.

The tradition of a common refectory and common recital of the Office was also being ignored, due to the exemptions allowed those who were away preaching or teaching, and the honours that accrued to those in the academic world, dispensing them from the common life and the common lot. General Chapters prohibited 'feasting in the dormitories', so obviously enclosure was also in jeopardy with the comings and goings of numerous lay people. Perhaps it was all this feasting in dormitories that led to poor attendance in the refectory, where maybe the cook was not as well qualified as one might desire! The eremitical roots of Carmel were thus imperceptibly eroded.

The Black Death which swept through Europe in the fourteenth and fifteenth centuries drastically decimated communities. There was a general relaxation of discipline and, to replenish the ranks of the departed, unsuitable candidates were too easily accepted. Carmel suffered along with all the other Orders of the period.

There were two ways of dealing with this spiritual malaise, the first being reform movements which sprang up spontaneously and were generally limited to certain houses or areas. In reformed friaries discipline was strict, poverty upheld and the spirit of retirement and prayer promoted. The other way, not necessarily contrary but rather complementary, was to seek mitigations of the Rule in order to meet the new circumstances that had arisen. The thinking behind the second alternative was that it was better for all to observe an 'observable' Rule than to disregard the Rule altogether because it made seemingly impossible demands.

In 1432 therefore the pope granted permission for Carmelites to be dispensed from continual presence in their cells (when not attending to other duties) and allowed them 'to walk about in the churches, cloisters and grounds'. They were also dispensed from abstinence three days a week except in Lent and Advent. One of the Generals of the Order, John Soreth, interpreted the mitigation as follows: 'To remove the scruples of the weak this has been declared by Eugene IV to mean that it is permitted to remain and freely walk about in churches, cloisters and convent precincts, meditating on the Law of the Lord and praying and serving in proper occupations'. In fact, mitigation was not an endorsement of laxity *per se*, it was the application of common sense to the current dilemma.

As regards food, fish was often unavailable and meat the only practical alternative. Poverty demanded that they accept whatever was cheap and easy to obtain. Permission had been granted for this in some provinces before the mitigation came into force; the English, for example, already had it in 1396.

But it would be well for the friars to have, within the Order itself, those who would embody poverty, community and prayer in a radical way; people who would keep these elements of the charism alive, challenging all to live more fully and generously the life they had professed.

The means proved to be the foundation of communities of nuns, for up until this time full membership of the Order had been limited to men. Some women seem to have been affiliated as confraternity members who were privileged to share in the spiritual benefits of Carmel and were permitted to wear the white mantle on certain ceremonial occasions (hence the term *mantellate*). Other individuals made an act of profession while continuing to live celibate lives in their own homes or occasionally in groups. But all these were peripheral to the main body of the Order which consisted of friars only.

The first extant act of oblation or profession of a woman is that of Sr Benevenuta Rainieri at Bologna in 1304. A few other professions are recorded, including accounts of women who lived as anchoresses attached to Carmelite churches. Such a one was Blessed Joan of Toulouse who lived in that city beside the Carmelite house, praying continually and edifying all. A contemporary of Julian of Norwich, Emma Stapleton, was a recluse beside the Carmelite friary in Norwich, and there were others. But all these were isolated cases, not the general norm. Carmel had no formally established communities of women, no official place for them in her legislation and thinking.

The first women were fully incorporated into the Order in 1452 when Pope Nicholas V granted the Bull *Cum nulla*, giving to the Prior General and provincials of the Carmelite Order the same privileges as the Franciscans and Dominicans with regard to 'the reception, way of life and admission of religious virgins, widows, beguines and *mantellate*' who, singly or in groups, would now or in the future present themselves for the protection of the Carmelite Order and wear its habit. John Soreth, who was Prior General at the time, was the protector of several groups of beguines and *mantellate* and he was keen to extend their influence and set them on a proper canonical footing. Without women he felt that the Order was incomplete.

It may seem strange that Carmel, with its Marian spirituality, had specifically avoided the inclusion of women into the Order as full members until now, and had indeed obtained a dispensation from anything to do with nuns. This is even more surprising in that the Franciscans, Dominicans and Augustinians had, almost from their inception, encouraged complementary communities of the opposite sex. They were considered an essential part of their Orders and were formed in the Order's spirituality while living enclosed lives of prayer, in contrast to that of their male counterparts engaged in apostolic works.

It may be that part of the trouble for the Carmelites was the same as for St Bernard and the Cistercians. It is all very well to sing the glories of Mary, that ideal woman; quite another to deal with actual women, who are not mere projections of the feminine ideal but persons in their own right, with all the limitations and particularities implied therein.

Women in religious life had a long history before any sisters became part of Carmel. In the seventh and eighth centuries there were many powerful monasteries of women in the Anglo-Saxon and Merovingian kingdoms. A monastery was considered a suitably dignified retreat for unmarried women and widows for whom society had no place. It was common practice then for wealthy families to establish and endow a foundation where the needs of a daughter or sister who could not, or would not marry, might be met. These ladies, coming as they did from the ruling classes, wielded considerable power. In a joint monastery of men and women it was customary for the abbess to govern, the men being appendages to provide sacramental ministry for the nuns and do the heavier manual work. Such were the great monasteries of Hilda of Whitby and Etheldreda of Ely in England, Radegunde in France. Here the abbess sat in on the councils of the powerful of the land and was revered for her wisdom. But as society became better organised male dominance reasserted itself.

From the tenth to twelfth centuries, the great period of monastic expansion, few double monasteries continued. Most were single sex, and foundations for men far outnumbered those for women. If double monasteries were inaugurated, this time it was the men who ruled, such as with the Gilbertines. Elsewhere a reaction quickly set in to exclude women altogether. The Premonstratentions, who had begun by admitting women, refused to take any more, viewing them as a source of temptation, to be avoided 'like poisonous animals'.

The Cistercian Order definitely did not want a feminine appendage, but women forced their way into the organisation anyway. With the connivance of individual abbots, Cistercian monasteries of women established themselves, following the customs and practices of Cîteaux but outside the highly controlled and centralised government which legislated for the men. Such was the monastery of Helfta in Saxony which nurtured such great scholars and mystics as St Mechtilde and St Gertrude the Great.

As more aristocratic ladies joined the Cistercian houses and found ways of nourishing themselves on Cistercian teaching, they also allowed themselves a great deal of liberty. By the time the Cistercian General Chapter took official notice of them it was too late. They had enjoyed their independence and were in no mood for restrictions imposed by a body in which they had no voice. The high-spirited abbess and nuns of Parc-aux-Dames in Northern France shouted and stamped and walked out of the Chapter house when the official visitor of the Order informed them of recent restrictive legislation.[1] It was a struggle (ultimately won by the monks) between very rich, high-born women who were determined to resist interference in their chosen lifestyle, and a legislative body that was forced unwillingly to take note of their presence and curb their freedom.

But the women who would eventually become the first nuns of the Carmelite Order are not to be traced to the strata of society that nurtured the nuns of the great abbeys of St Benedict and St Bernard. They were from a quite separate movement, springing from a different social class – that of the beguines.

The beguines seem to have originated in Liege about 1210 and from there spread throughout Flanders and hence to Germany, Bohemia and all northern Europe. They were specifically a feminine phenomenon, not an outgrowth of an established male Order.

The beguines arose as a way of dealing with the surplus women of the cities, many left widows by the crusading fever that swept the men off to the Holy Land to fight the Infidel.

The term 'beguine' is thought to have arisen as a term of contempt, a contraction of the word 'Albigensian', detractors saying that these women wished to be thought of, and claimed to be, holier than others. However, attempts to smear the beguines as heretics failed, and in the main they were recognised as right living and of orthodox faith.

The women who joined the movement came generally from the rising middle class. They were not wealthy or aristocratic enough to find a place in the older Orders where substantial dowries were required, nor did they relish the status of lay sisters in such establishments where they would be little more than glorified servants. Beguines were widows, sisters, daughters, of respectable burghers, skilled artisans and lesser knights. They had a modicum of money and learning, were capable, thrifty and willing to play a part in religious life without relinquishing too much of their dearly acquired independence. Alone, they were prey to a society that took little note of women; together they could forge a future for themselves according to their own plans.

Beguines were not nuns but religious 'sisters', using the term in its broadest sense. They did not make permanent vows, had no universal rule of life, no one founder, no outside authority. Each group, with amazing flexibility, decided on a lifestyle according to the perceived needs of time and place in which the sisters found themselves. Beguines might live together in a common dwelling, performing some work of charity such as nursing or visiting the poor; others had their own separate little house within a compound (an example of the erstwhile separate cells of the medieval Carmelites at Aylesford would give a good idea of how some beguinages made use of a common dwelling with separate entrances for each sister), others lived in their own homes. A wide choice was available with the minimum of complications. Forms of commitment also varied. The usual procedure was for the aspirant to appear before her parish priest or some other authorised ecclesiastic and declare her intention to live a religious life after the manner of a beguine. Following the celebration of Mass the woman made her profession and was offered a religious dress which she promised to wear as a person dedicated to God. If the intending beguine was a woman whose husband had gone on a Crusade she would only remain in the beguinage during his absence and was free to rejoin him if and when he returned from the war.

Employments for beguines were various. Earning a living was considered an essential part of the life, in contrast to the 'holy leisure' of the traditional nun. There was hospital work, embroidery, instructing young girls, domestic tasks, with simple prayer and meditation underpinning the daily labour.

The beguines spread rapidly, their popularity reaching its zenith in the late thirteenth century. Relative freedom of movement and the fact that beguines could develop their own prayer life led them in many cases to attach themselves to communities of mendicants. Beguines were to be found in the vicinity of many Franciscan and Dominican houses where the friars would act as spiritual directors.

However, it was not long before the very popularity of the beguines led to a reaction. People resented their freedom from cloister and strict obedience. It was said that these women should either marry or enter an approved Order. The Council of Vienne in 1312 tried to suppress the movement even though in the end it had to admit that women who followed a chaste, religious way of life, supported by devotion to God and service to their neighbour, should be allowed to do so unmolested. But suspicion continued and most beguines, to allay further difficulties, affiliated themselves to established Orders, mostly the mendicants which, in the case of the Franciscans and Dominicans, had regular Tertiaries of similar lifestyle fully approved by the Church. Some independent groups of beguines continued, but the first impulse had been lost.

Similar communities of women in Italy and Spain, termed *mantellate* or *beatas* respectively, also tried to find and hold some place within the structures of religious life with more or less degrees of success, though these were never as numerous or independent-minded as the beguines of Germany and the Low Countries.

It was at this point that John Soreth, the reforming General of the Carmelites, came on the scene. Soreth was born at Caen in Normandy in 1394 when Normandy was still under British rule (remaining so until 1450). He received his doctorate in Paris in 1438 and from 1440 to 1450, when he was elected General, was head of the Province. Eager to initiate reforms in the Order, Soreth produced new Constitutions for the men and was the first to provide for women, something for which he will always be remembered. Women added a new dimension to Carmel that was to endure, even though the beginnings were small.

In 1452 the very first community of Carmelite nuns was admitted to the Order through Soreth's instrumentality. They were the beguines of Ten Elsen in the Netherlands. Soreth placed them under the jurisdiction of the prior of Guelders who was to provide them with the religious habit and a way of life suitable to the circumstances of persons and place. Later Soreth himself wrote Statutes for these nuns, which unfortunately have not been preserved.

The same year, a community of *mantellate* in Florence received a smiliar privilege from the Carmelite prior of that city who had journeyed to Rome to receive the Bull *Cum nulla* on their behalf.

From this point on we find other beguine groups joining the Order in the Low Countries, and Carmelite priors providing for their instruction in the Order's spirituality. The men applied the Rule and Constitutions to them, with adaptations for women, incorporating such practices as enclosure, common life, the recitation of the Divine Office and manual labour.

Neukirke, Dinant, Liege, Vilvoorde, all were former beguine foundations which came under Soreth's direction. Other houses developed independently or were initiated by local priors. In France, sisterhoods were established through the efforts of Blessed Frances d'Amboise, Duchess of Brittany. She met Soreth after being recently widowed and was one of the very few aristocrats to join the early movement and enter Carmel, endowing her monasteries from her own patrimony and ruling as prioress for many years.

While the communities under Soreth's direct influence seem to have observed enclosure and lived a regular life consistent with customary coventual discipline, those communities which evolved from groups of *mantellate* and *beatas* in Italy and Spain were less traditional. Some kept enclosure, some were more free. There was still no central authority, no strong woman who could give this specific vocation within the Order a voice and direction.

Who then were these first sisters of Ten Elsen or Dinant? What were they like? What did they think? What contribution did they make to their own form of life as they adapted from being beguines to being nuns? How did they interpret the Carmelite charism in their own situation? These questions are no longer answerable. The beguines-turned-Carmelites are as anonymous as the early hermits on Mount Carmel. We can picture them as in the paintings of a Van Eyke or a Memling: their faces inscrutable, hidden in the white coifs which framed their features, their hands beneath their newly donned scapulars, their white mantles falling in graceful folds to the floor of their choir as they struggled, with their limited education, to master the Sacred Liturgy according to the Carmelite Rite of the Holy Sepulchre. These are women taking on the task of re-interpreting an old tradition, anonymous women sinking their roots deep into Carmel's soil to become a praying, Marian presence. They form the humus from which would spring the greatest of all Carmelite women, Teresa of Avila, but also many more now revered throughout the universal church: Mary Magdalen of Pazzi, Thérèse of Lisieux, Elizabeth of the Trinity, Edith Stein. These latter do not, cannot stand without the former, any more than the Carmelite Order can reckon without its original anonymous hermits established in the Wadi es Siah.

The first women of Carmel, as they endeavoured to find their identity, were not 'great souls'. They were, in the main, practical women, barely educated, ready to earn a living in whatever way they could within the enclosure. Often they had not originally chosen this lifestyle. They found themselves in it through circumstances which decreed that their survival as a community depended on their affiliation to an established Order.

Growing, searching, dependent on Carmelite priors who followed a different way of life, the nuns' path must often have seemed unclear, winding, suffering. But they carried on silently, digging and harrowing and planting the soil in their small area, recalling their spiritual orientation in the dedication of their houses: Our Lady of Jerusalem, Our Lady of Sion, the Three Maries, Our Lady of Nazareth, St Mary of the Angels, St Mary of Paradise ... The Mother of God was with them in their hidden self-effacement. That sufficed.

From such insignificant beginnings these first nuns opened the horizons of Carmel for women, so that years later Thérèse of Lisieux could sing of the freedom and joy found within the enclosure notwithstanding all its attendant restrictions:

> Jesus, your love is always present with me;
> in you I have the woods, the countryside,
> I have the rose bushes, the distant mountains,
> the rain and the flakes of snow
> from the heavens.
>
> In you I have rivulets and hillocks,
> lianas, periwinkle, hawthorne,
> fresh water lilies, honeysuckle, eglantines,
> the soft rustling of the slender poplar trees.
>
> Oh, you who support all these worlds,
> who plant the thick forests
> and render them fertile with a single glance,
> you follow me with a look of loving care
> continually.

Enclosure, which expresses one aspect of the hermit tradition of Carmel and which is more pronounced in the life of the nuns, is not meant to be an evasion of reality. Rather, it is a more intense form of living, simply because it is confined to the limited world of the same house, grounds and companions, without the distractions and 'escapes' available to people outside. Everyone's world is limited by *some* boundaries; in enclosure these boundaries are freely chosen. However, life is life wherever it is lived, with all its potential for growth and depths, for relationships and for inner development.

The enclosure of Carmel has to provide room for many different people to grow. It must provide for different temperaments, for emotional and intellectual needs, and for the muddle and contradictions that are part of everyday life as it forges Godwards. Enclosure is not an antiseptic environment but a richly human one. Only in and through our humanity can we come to God, who has entered fully into our human condition and made it his own.

If enclosure narrows and constricts the person it is useless. Carmel is a country of infinite horizons, 'the best country in the world' as Elizabeth of the Trinity wrote. It is a country that opens up vistas of prayer but also vistas of the human condition and the human heart that are often left untouched by those who shy away from reality.

Prayer unites people at their deepest level of pain, bewilderment and sorrow. The one who lives her prayer is therefore a person who experiences her own humanity and silently makes it fruitful for others. This is an indispensable part of Carmel, and only with the advent of the women did the Order really bear explicit witness to this truth and thus become whole.

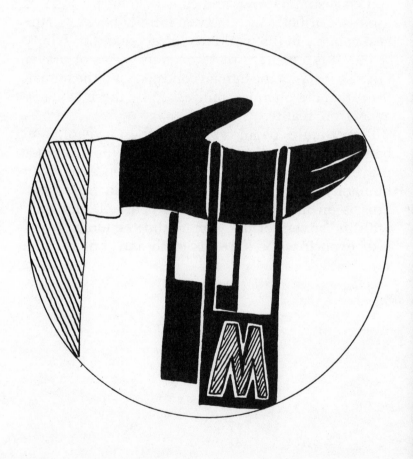

CHAPTER EIGHT

CLOTHING AND CONTEMPLATION FOR ALL

With women established as full members of the Order it was time to extend formal affiliation to all who desired to associate themselves with Carmel, whatever their manner of life. The official Third Order for lay people was contemporaneous with the foundation of the nuns, but another form of incorporation that has achieved widespread popularity is the wearing of the brown scapular. This consists of two pieces of brown cloth joined by tapes over the shoulders and worn under ordinary clothes. It is a mini-habit, a piece of the land of Carmel for everyone.

The wearing of a religious habit identifies a person as a member of a certain group, living within a definite spiritual tradition. The full habit is reserved for professed members of the Order, but we have seen that from quite early on confraternities of lay people might be attached to a Carmelite church. These men and women wanted to proclaim their love for Our Lady of Mount Carmel by wearing the white mantle in her honour on certain ceremonial occasions. Others were designated as *laudesi* (Marian hymn singers) and received the same privilege.

This outward sign of attachment to the Carmelite

Order was very popular, but a mantle is a heavy, cumbersome garment, not worn as part of one's ordinary clothing. What of daily life? Something was needed that would remind people continually of their dedication to Mary in the same way as the friars and nuns wore the religious habit when about their ordinary tasks. The answer was to symbolise the whole habit by a small piece of it, the scapular.

The scapular, originally an apron, was part of the religious garb of most Orders. It consisted of two pieces of cloth that hung down over the front and back of the habit 'proper' – tunic and belt. But within a very short time the scapular had lost its practical function as an apron and had been incorporated into the habit itself, a symbol of the sweet yoke of Christ which religious took upon themselves by their vows of poverty, chastity and obedience. The Benedictines wore a black scapular, the Dominicans a white one. Other Orders also adopted the scapular as a form of dress, often proclaiming their particular identity with some further decoration, such as a red cross emblazoned on the front.

The Carmelites had originally worn a habit and scapular of undyed wool which was greyish brown. Later a black habit was the norm, and finally it ended up as dark brown, the familiar colour today. In a smaller version, the scapular could be worn under lay clothing; it was discreet, cheap, convenient, and a sign of affiliation with the Order. As 'Mary's habit' it assumed a special significance, legend attributing to St Simon Stock a promise from the Virgin herself that those who wore the scapular were placing themselves under her special protection and would be assured of attaining heaven.

The custom of pushing traditions back and back to an ever earlier date is common. This particular tradition was linked to the changing of the Order from a hermit lifestyle to that of a mendicant one, and Mary's promise to be with the friars in their new orientation. But however the story originated (and it certainly does *not* date from the thirteenth century) the scapular has been the means of giving many people a link with Carmel that they value and cherish. It is popular piety in the literal sense, a sacramental for everyone. It places the wearer under the patronage of Mary and is a reminder of the interior life which is pre-eminently Marian.

The devotional wearing of the scapular rather than the mantle was popularised by John Baptist Rossi, General of the Carmelites from 1564–1578, at the time when St Teresa was busy founding her reformed convents of nuns in Spain; but the custom of giving lay people part of the habit can be traced to the *laudesi, mantellate*, and others who viewed the Carmelite habit as a sign of devotion to the Mother of God and wanted to be associated with the Order by some visible token.

Clothes have always held a significant place in human society because in most countries they are a basic requirement for survival, an elemental need. Clothes express our understanding of who we are and who we want to be. They are an extension of the personality, expressing as they do our sense of personal dignity and our role in society. In relating to the rest of the human community we often use terms associated with dress. We speak of blue and white collar workers, of city dress and evening dress. There is a different form of dress for work and for leisure, for the young and for the old.

In the Old Testament the use of clothes reflects God's creation, drawing order out of chaos, adorning and making fertile. As God separates the opposites in creation: darkness and light, the waters above and below the firmament, the ocean and dry land, so clothing separates male and female, priest and layperson, Jew and gentile.

As God gives vegetation to beautify the earth, the sun, moon and stars to adorn the heavens, so clothes beautify the wearer. When Isaac woos Rebecca he sends bridal gifts through the hands of his servant 'jewellery of silver and gold, and garments' (Gen. 24:52). The Lord likewise gifts Israel his bride with 'the garments of salvation and the robe of righteousness' (Is. 61:10).

God also makes fertile, giving the command to increase and multiply. So in all societies there is a sexual meaning in clothes. To be clothed by a husband is a symbol of brideship, as when Boaz spreads his mantle over Ruth as she sleeps at his feet during the night of the Bethlehem barley harvest (Rt. 3:9), or as the Lord clothes Jerusalem when he chooses her as his own city and raises her from obscurity to queenship (Ez. 16:8).

The Office of the Immaculate Conception speaks of Mary as the one robed in grace from head to foot: gifted and loved in a way that is totally unmerited. This is the source of her joy and her song, the *Magnificat*.

While clothes protect the dignity of a person, nakedness in the bible is the sign of being an 'outsider'. To clothe the naked is to bring them into the human community, it is to do for others what God has done for us (Is. 58:7).

The Baptismal robe of Christians is given after the stripping and descent into the water, so that symbolically one rises as a new person. One 'puts on Christ' in the white garment, leaving behind the darkness of sin. To be clothed with Christ is to be translated into a wholly new manner of living:

As God's chosen ones, holy and beloved, clothe yourselves with compassion, kindness, humility, meekness and patience. Bear with one another, and if anyone has a complaint against another, forgive each other; just as the Lord has forgiven you, so you also must forgive. Above all, clothe yourselves with love, which binds everything together in perfect harmony. And let the peace of Christ rule in your hearts, to which indeed you were called in one body. And be thankful.

Let the word of Christ dwell in you richly; teach each other and admonish one another in all wisdom; and with gratitude in your hearts sing psalms, hymns and spiritual songs to God. And whatever you do, in word or deed, do everything in the name of the Lord Jesus, giving thanks to God the Father through him.

(Col. 3:12–17)

The Church, dealing as she does in the language of signs and symbols, blesses the religious habit as a sign of consecration in view of the resurrection of the whole body-person. By putting on the habit of a particular Order one shows in an external manner that one is wanting to be conformed interiorly to a particular spirituality. One is being set within a tradition of common life, expressing that incorporation by adopting a certain mode of dress. 'All we who wear the holy habit of the Carmelites are called to prayer and contemplation' writes Teresa of Avila, 'that was the first principle of our Order. We are descended from those holy ancestors of ours from Mount Carmel who sought this treasure, this precious pearl of which we speak'.

Carmel is indeed the Order of prayer, but it is a prayer that is open to everyone because it is a Marian way of being. Mary, as model of life and prayer, introduces her children to prayer through ways that are ordinary and homely, as ordinary and homely and straightforward as the wearing of a simple garment like the brown scapular.

It is the prerogative of a mother to clothe her family. Hannah, Samuel's mother, asserts her maternity by continuing to bring her son a little robe every year (I Sam. 2:19) even though he is now living away from home in the service of Eli the priest. The good wife clothes her household well, and this sign of concern is a motive for others to praise her industry. The clothing she provides is both literal and figurative in meaning:

> She puts her hands to the distaff
> and her hands hold the spindle.
> She opens her hands to the poor
> and reaches out her hands to the needy.
> She is not afraid for her household when it snows,
> for all her household are clothed in crimson.
> She makes herself coverings,
> her clothing is of fine linen and purple.
> Her husband is known at the city gates
> taking his seat among the elders of the land.
> She makes linen garments and sells them;
> she supplies the merchant with sashes.
> Strength and dignity are her clothing,
> and she laughs at the time to come.
> She opens her mouth with wisdom,
> and the teaching of kindness is on her tongue.
> She looks well to the ways of her household,
> and does not eat the bread of idleness.
>   (Prov. 30:19–27)

Mary, as mother, would have wrapped Jesus in the

swaddling bands she had made to receive him when he was born. She would have prepared the festive garments for his Bar Mizvah when he first journeyed to Jerusalem as a 'son of the Law', accepting thereby the responsibility of an adult male Jew to live by the Covenant offered to Abraham and Moses. Jesus would have worn the fringes, or tassels, prescribed by the Law, and Mary would certainly have seen to it that he dressed as befitted one of the chosen people.

The Lord said to Moses:

Speak to the Israelites and tell them to make fringes on the corners of their garments throughout their generations and to put a blue cord on the fringe at each corner. You have the fringe so that when you see it you will remember all the commandments of the Lord and do them, and not follow the lust of your own heart or your own eyes. So you shall remember and do all my commandments and you shall be holy to your God.

(Num. 15:37–40)

The clothing of the Jews was a continual reminder that they belonged to God in a special way. The woman with a haemorrhage who reached out to touch the hem of Christ's garment was grasping the tassels shot through with blue cord as prescribed by the Law.

At the last, standing beneath the cross, Mary would have seen the soldiers cast lots for the privilege of receiving her Son's seamless tunic, woven in one piece by her diligent hands but now cast on the ground, stained and sodden. When he died the small four-cornered ritual garment of the Israelite would have fluttered on his agonising body as he inaugurated the New Covenant in his blood.

In his novel *Mary*, the Jewish writer, Scholem Asch, depicts Mary on her way to Gesthemane accompanied in spirit by the biblical Rachel. Mary is overwhelmed with grief, having a foreboding of her Son's approaching agony, and she begs that he might be spared at the prayers of his mother. At this point Rachel speaks to her as follows:

> My child, I too wished to be no more than a mother. But when Jacob came to Paddan-aran, and single handed rolled the stone from the well's mouth to water my flock, he lifted the stone that lay over the mouth of the future, revealing to me the destinies of Israel unto the end of days. And when he kissed my mouth and lifted up his voice and wept, his tears quickened in me the springs of compassion. In his tears I forefelt the agony of Israel, gored like a lamb by the beasts of the field, driven from exile to exile. In his sobs I heard Israel treading the way of its sorrows unto the day of redemption. For Jacob wept with the tears of a father and sanctified me to be the mother of Israel's grief. And thus I was made the mother of the children of Israel.[1]

'I too wished to be no more than a mother.' Mary had known the mystery of childbirth, the warmth of new life growing within her, the joys and apprehensions that belong to parenthood. Yet that was not enough. Like Rachel of old, Mary had to learn that her destiny was more than some private domestic idyll. Through her Son she would be led to a compassion that embraced not only Israel but the whole world.

In the book, Rachel next shows Mary a great field and, as she looks more closely, it seems to be sown with eyes, all looking towards her, pleading for her to let her Son go so that he might be the Redeemer of all.

For Mary to hold him back for herself would be to ignore the pleas of the suffering. And thus she consents to release Jesus, that he may fulfil his destiny, so closely linked with hers as his mother.

Mary was there beneath the cross at the end, but she was present on Calvary only because in the preceding years she had walked the path of contemplation in daily life, as we all have to do if we take our faith seriously.

Through Mary, Jesus became one of us. What a mystery! The Son of God born from a woman's body like any other baby. He had to be fed and changed, cuddled and clothed. His mother had to teach him his prayers and his table manners like any other small child.

In the Virgin of Carmel, queen of contemplatives, who invites us to be one with her in her pondering and praying, we see a woman doing the work of her contemporaries, being nothing 'special' at all. On the surface it doesn't add up. How can Mary have such an exalted title when she appears to be so ordinary? It becomes clear only if we look more deeply and with the eyes of faith.

In the gospel for the feast of Our Lady of Mount Carmel we do not see Mary on that mountain famed for its beauty, but on another mountain, Mount Calvary. Here Jesus gives her to be mother of us all. Here we see her in her true fruitfulness as her Son's heart is opened to release the waters of the Spirit. Jesus shows us what love means, what love costs, if we persevere to the end.

To be a contemplative like Mary is to be attuned to suffering in that it means being open and sensitive to the demands of life, of reality. It is about living in the dimension of faith here and now. To be a contemplative is to be 'love in the heart of the church', and that is no esoteric attainment beyond the reach of every-day people and everyday life.

In Mary we see the true contemplative, the true lover. And as she is the image of the Church she is the image of what each one of us is called to be. The canonical contemplative-apostolic life as lived by the friars and nuns of Carmel is one way to be Christian, to be Marian, but it is only *one* way. Mary shows us that to which *all* can aspire, whatever their vocation. We are to be one with her, whether it be at Nazareth or Jerusalem, Calvary or Carmel.

When we look at Mary as the gospels portray her, we see three qualities on which we can focus, qualities that are worth pondering and are not confined to any one form of life. They are the qualities of attentiveness, freedom and service.

Firstly, one of the key things Mary teaches us is attentiveness, that inner attitude vital to contemplation. Scripture shows her as completely attentive both to the divine and human elements in her life.

At the Annunciation Mary is depicted as a woman who is alert, listening, questioning. She wants to know, to see the situation as clearly as possible. She wants to welcome the truth and play her part in salvation history with full consent. She is therefore attentive to the words of the angel who comes as God's messenger.

But she does not rest there. Mary is attentive also on the human level. She does not sit musing quietly over what has transpired. She rises and goes to her elderly relative who might need help.

At Cana Mary is attentive, not just to the presence and words of Jesus but to the possible embarrassment of a newly-married couple. The wine of Heaven and the wine of earth intermingle in her actions and words.

This quality of attentiveness, of discreet, self-effacing vigilance, is characteristic of a prayerful, contemplative life. It is the essence of Mary's life and can, indeed should, be the essence of our own, whether in the world or in the cloister. If we are attentive, pondering all things in our heart, we will be able to act with wisdom.

The second quality Mary teaches us is freedom or non-attachment. Mary is perfectly present to God and to others because she is attached to nothing except God and God's will. Mary is free. She is not holding on to preconceived ideas of how things *ought* to be; rather she sees things as they actually *are*. She is, as St John of the Cross says, completely transparent.

Mary is not ensnared in thoughts about herself, her opinions, the results of her actions. Her whole attitude is 'Behold the handmaid of the Lord, be it done to me according to *your* word' – not mine.

Mary is able to respond to the needs of the moment because she is not clinging anxiously to the past or thinking fearfully about the future. Neither does she cling to her Son or try to force him into some pattern of her own choosing. She allows Jesus to be free as she herself struggles to be free, even when that freedom culminates in the cross. True love always allows the other to be free, even at cost to oneself.

And lastly, the other side of the coin of freedom is, surprisingly perhaps, practical action, the ability to give help however and wherever it is needed, and what could be more down-to-earth than that.

The great temptation of so-called 'spiritual people' is lack of involvement in life's nitty gritty. That is not the case with Mary, perfect contemplative that she is. To be a pray-er has nothing to do with being woolly and unfocused. Through the Incarnation God has chosen to immerse himself in the world of human relationships and human concerns. Nothing is too small or insignificant for him, even two sparrows sold for a farthing.

And so we see Mary reflecting the caring, heavenly Father. She cares, and is not just carried away by flights of fancy.

Whenever Mary appears in the Gospel we find her doing whatever is possible in the concrete circumstances in which she finds herself. It is the natural outcome of her closeness to God in prayer. Although the Bethlehem stable was presumably not what she would have chosen as the setting for her confinement, Luke simply records that she wrapped Jesus in swaddling clothes and laid him in a manger. She did the best she could with what was available. And although she did not know it at the time, this practical, loving realism at the beginning of Jesus' life was one of the small steps preparing her to do all that had to be done at the end, even if she could only stand helplessly beneath the cross ready, when all was accomplished, to receive him into her arms once more and wrap him in grave clothes ready to be placed in the tomb.

Motherhood is a supremely practical activity. It takes discipline, self-forgetfulness, sensitivity and active love. It begins with people close at hand – in home, family and community, and from there it embraces the world.

One who wants to imitate Mary lives like her in the NOW – attentive, present to God and others, ready to do in any small way whatever needs doing.

Baron von Hugel wrote that 'in modern society only the mystic will survive'. He had in mind, no doubt, not only his cloistered Carmelite daughter but everyone who takes the Christian life seriously. At first reading one could be left thinking that one had missed the challenge; but if we look at Mary we realise that to be a mystic is simply to live like her. She, above all, is the one who loved and followed her Son perfectly.

In the book *The Cardinal* we find the portrayal of a dedicated young woman, Lalage Menton. Lalage is an icon of Mary, revealing as she does to Stephen, the newly ordained priest, something of what it means to be truly concerned for others as she sets about clothing the figures in the parish crib:

Late one afternoon, a couple of days before Christmas, Stephen entered the church, thinking to make a happier arrangement of the crèche. In the crimson light flowing from the sanctuary lamp, he saw a young woman bending over the crib; her posture was that of a mother putting her child to bed, and she murmured softly as she tucked and patted the figure in the manger. At her feet was a pile of hay.

Only one woman in the world could bestow such comfort and order with her bare hands.

'Lalage!'

The girl turned. Wisps of hay were in her chestnut hair. The hay was timothy, and its perfume hung field-sweet above Lalage Menton's face.

'I hope you don't mind what I'm doing to your crèche' she said.

'What are you doing?'

'Just making it into a stable. It was a stable, remember? With hay.' She stuffed handfuls of fragrant clover under the oxen, making them appear to be munching contemplatively at the wonder before them. Lalage tucked more hay about the kneeling figure of Mary, softening the edges of her blue robe and bringing her an inch nearer the child. 'There – she looks more comfortable, don't you think?'

'Yes, she does.' Stephen marvelled at Lalage's way with things living or inanimate. 'But what's that you're putting on St Joseph?'

'It's chilly in here, said Lalage, 'so I made him a little sheepskin vest.' She slipped the garment over the carpenter-saint's shoulders, kissed the back of his patient neck. 'All we need now is a bellyband for the Infant.'

Stephen found himself vetoing the bellyband. 'I'm afraid' he said, 'that a touch like that would make things too naturalistic. After all, the crèche is intended to suggest what happened that first Christmas night. The hay helps carry out that suggestion – it was just the thing we needed. But if we get too realistic – with a vest for Joseph and a bellyband for the Christ-child – we're apt to lose sight of what the characters stand for.'

Lalage gazed at the three principal figures as if trying to grasp the meaning beyond them. 'I forgot they stood for anything' she said. 'I keep thinking of them as people in a cold barn.'

Lalage Menton's ideas about the Incarnation might bring smiles or even frowns to a synod of bishops, but Stephen realised that she was the bearer of something much more important – the special love that is the monopoly of women.[2]

Later, Lalage confides to Stephen that she is about to join the Geraldines, a community specialising in the nursing of incurables. This is the burden she is taking on, and *wants* to take on, because she believes it is the burden she has been born to carry.

So this was the secret of Lalage's wide open heart, her mystifying habit of walking up to life with outstretched arms! Stephen understood now the hidden source from which her actions bubbled. Strong in vocation, dedicated to purity, she could pour affectionate strength over everything she encountered: a braggart father, a spavined horse, a whittled wooden figure of St Joseph, a fellow-creature wasting incurably to death – or a priest, endangered perhaps by a too stuffy reading of his role. All needy things claimed her, and she responded in proportion to their want. Everything Lalage Menton did or said was only a manifestation of the thing she was.[3]

To be Marian, to wear the scapular of Carmel, is to wear the apron of service, of love, of being a Marian presence in the world. It is for *everyone*. To put on the scapular is not only to declare one's affiliation with the Carmelite Order but to claim one's own part in the life of prayer that Carmel signifies.

To be a living icon of Mary, the Christ-bearer, is one of the ideals of the Carmelite. And, as with Wisdom personified, the discipline of love and service leads one to be clothed with a personality that reflects the woman who embodies Wisdom in all her actions:

> For wisdom is like her name;
> she is not readily perceived by many.
> Put your feet into her fetters and your neck into
>   her collar.
> Bend your shoulders and carry her
> and do not fret under her bonds.
> Come to her with all your soul
> and keep her ways with all your might.
> Search out and seek her, and she will become
>   known to you,
> and when you get hold of her do not let her go.
> For at last you will find the rest she gives,

and she will be changed into joy for you.
Then her fetters will become for you a strong
     defence,
and her collar a glorious robe.
Her yoke is a golden ornament and her bonds are
     purple cord.
You will wear her like a glorious robe
and put her on like a splendid crown.

(Sir. 6:22–31)

CHAPTER NINE

LA MADRE

It can happen occasionally in the life of an Order that one or two supremely gifted people are able to interpret the charism and live it with such vibrancy and originality that they leave a permanent legacy behind them – not only for the Order but for the whole church. Such are Teresa of Avila and John of the Cross. Their names have become identified with Carmel in such a way that any account of the charism would be incomplete without them. In their lives and teaching they reveal much of the richness latent in Carmelite spirituality that was only waiting to be articulated. As reformers they returned to the original inspiration of the first hermits but they also incorporated all that had been learned and lived by others during the period that followed the migration to the West.

What kind of woman was Teresa? Certainly she was not the mild, obedient nun of pious fiction. She was a woman of genius, very much an individual – in Jungian terminology a 'self-actuating' woman. She was balanced, humorous, gifted with immense courage and foresight, no respector of persons, a leader in every way. Yet her early years gave little hint of what lay ahead for her as writer, teacher, foundress; one wholly given to God in her chosen vocation.

Teresa was born in 1515 in Avila, Spain. She was the third child of her father's second marriage, one of a large family, twelve in all. Her grandfather had been a Jew, Juan Sanchez, a silk merchant from Toledo who was forcibly converted at the time of the Spanish Inquisition. Publicily paraded in the infamous *sanbenitas* (penitential garments) at Toledo cathedral he, with his sons, one of whom, Alonso, was to become Teresa's father, moved to Avila to escape the taint still attached to *conversos*. There he married into an unassailably Catholic family, the Cepedas. Most of Alonso's family retained the de Cepeda name, which ensured their acceptance as unquestionably catholic and aristocratic, but Alonso's two daughters by his second marriage to Beatriz de Ahumada, Teresa and Juana, took their own mother's name in preference. Theirs was a fine, cultured household, rich and prosperous, at least during Teresa's childhood.

Teresa was gifted, lively, intelligent and vivacious, the acknowledged favourite of her father, assured of a brilliant marriage when she should reach the right age. However, it seems that Teresa was not particularly interested in marriage. She saw her own mother confined to the home, exhausted by frequent childbearing, and dying when her daughter was only fourteen. Teresa said Beatriz already looked like an old woman although she was still in her early thirties when death claimed her.

Freed temporarily from the constraints of feminine supervision Teresa now embarked on an adventurous adolescence (as far as was compatible with the vigilance exercised by Spaniards over their unmarried daughters, jealous to preserve the family honour at all costs). She flirted, enjoyed a secret 'affair', liked rich clothes and jewels, and indulged her vanity, making friends with some undesirable cousins who frequented her home as if it were their own.

Alonso grew alarmed. To counteract the influences that were dominating his daughter he sent Teresa to board with a community of Augustinian sisters who ran a school for the daughters of the Avilese nobility. While there, Teresa began to think that perhaps she should be a nun; not because she felt particularly attracted to the life but merely to save her soul. It was a decision of reason rather than emotion. Besides, the only other alternative was marriage, which would not suit someone of so independent a turn of mind. This was the era when a wife was supposed to show complete subservience to her husband!

Instead of joining the nuns who had educated her, Teresa decided on the Carmelite convent of the Incarnation in her native city. In her Autobiography she admits disarmingly that she chose the Carmelites because she had a friend there and the life was not too strict. It is possible too that her Jewish ancestry inclined her to a form of life that had originated in the East, for when Teresa entered Carmel the Elianic legends were firmly established as facts which Teresa would have taken for granted.

The Incarnation had been founded in 1479 by a group of single women living as *beatas* (the Spanish equivalent of beguines). The house had been duly aggregated to the Carmelite Order, its inhabitants gaining thereby the status of nuns without having had any formal training in a conventual way of life. Friars from the city acted as spiritual directors, but the Order in Spain was at a low ebb, remote as it was from reforms carried out in other parts of Europe.

The old *beatorio*, rebuilt in 1513, housed the

community which saw the entrance of the twenty year old Dona Teresa de Ahumada in 1535. True to form, when her father's consent was not forthcoming, she ran away from home with a brother while it was still dark on the eve of All Souls day, presenting herself at the convent and facing her father with a *fait accompli*. He, poor man, had to accept the inevitable. He loved his daughter, and proved it by setting her up in a private apartment comprising kitchen, guestroom, oratory and parlour. There was accommodation for friends to stay if they wished and an annuity to ensure that her material needs were met. The reasoning went that, if a daughter of Don Alonso must be a nun, let it at least be in keeping with her social status. Teresa saw no contradiction in the way of life she was professing and the provision made for her personal welfare. The situation was taken for granted and she was genuinely happy as her novitiate year progressed.

Teresa now embarked on a very ambivalent period of life which was to last for twenty years. She was pleased to have attained her goal. She had strong mindedly said that she wanted to be a nun and she was one, having surmounted the obstacles placed in her path by her family. She was a woman of honour who wanted to fulfil her obligations, but she was without proper discipline and guidance. The standards of the convent were low and there were over a hundred sisters within its walls.

Teresa desired to pray but other distractions were well-nigh overwhelming. She resided close to her home and her relatives, she was gifted for friendship, extremely attractive and much in demand in the parlours and at the houses of her numerous admirers. Even her burgeoning spirituality was a trap as it drew disciples to her who wished to learn about prayer. They kept her talking as if she were some kind of guru, whereas she knew herself that she would be more authentic did she but pray more and talk less. Besides, her poor health (most likely psychosomatic in origin as she suffered from many unidentified illnesses) prevented her from giving herself unreservedly to God, or so she thought. The convent did not observe strict enclosure, there was no apostolate of education or nursing which might have claimed Teresa's unfocused energy, and because of poverty and mismanagement of funds, the nuns without a private income were obliged to spend long periods away residing with relatives, if only to ensure some regular meals.

In such a situation Teresa was torn between obsvering religious discipline and following the path of pleasure; between the society of congenial companions and solitude with God. She was gifted with a rich interior life but her manner of living did not grow apace. When at prayer she watched the hour glass, longing to be back in the parlour. When in the parlour her conscience plagued her and she wished to return to prayer.

At last, in middle age, this double-mindedness ceased. She experienced a conversion before an image of the wounded Christ and determined to give herself to him unreservedly. It was the turning point of her life.

Having made a definitive decision in favour of the Lord, Teresa knew that her weakness needed the support of a proper environment. Backed by a few well-wishers she looked to the origins of the Carmelite Order as proposed in the Rule of St Albert, which she vowed to restore in its fulness, without mitigation.

It may be that Teresa was not cognisant with the Rule, even though her convent was officially under the Order's jurisdiction, but when she familiarised herself with its contents and spirit she felt within her a new sense of freedom and directedness. In the Rule she intuited the seeds of a vision for which she was longing. It contained an ideal of prayer and solitude that appealed to her radical nature. Teresa therefore resolved to follow the Rule as perfectly as possible and encouraged others to do likewise.

When Teresa realised that her dream would not be practicable, given the situation prevailing at the Incarnation, she decided, in her energetic way (and with some misgivings for she was already in her forties and loved her comfortable life and familiar quarters) to found a house where the eremitical spirit of Carmel could be revived. Strict enclosure would ensure that all energies could be devoted to the Lord, the nuns being 'not merely nuns but hermits'. Little had St Albert guessed that the Rule he had compiled for a small *laura* of recluses would provide the inspiration for what was to become the largest Order of contemplative nuns in the Catholic Church! I wonder too how this most proper of ecclesiastics would have viewed Teresa, a woman overflowing with vitality and enthusiasm and now proposing to lead the life of a 'hermit'.

Originally Teresa intended to establish only one convent but requests began to pour in for further foundations and she felt she could not refuse what she saw as a work of love for the church. She had no desire to begin a new Order, and she explicitly disclaimed the title of foundress. Instead she saw herself as one who was restoring Carmel's original emphasis on the primacy of prayer.

Teresa did not divorce prayer and apostolate. She saw prayer as the *contribution* of her nuns to the apostolate. They had no outside work to distract them and so they were to support the theologians and preachers by lives of holiness and self- sacrifice on behalf of those who fought in the thick of the fray.

Basic to mendicant and eremitical spirituality is the idea that anyone can come close to the Lord and enter into a deep relationship with him; this is not a privilege reserved for monks and nuns. Mendicants and hermits traditionally followed a more ordinary lifestyle, closer to people. They promoted relationships of equality among themselves rather than a feudal style of government. As we have seen, there was an emphasis on poverty, work, solitary prayer, a desire to bring others to the love of the Lord who had shared our human condition; taken on our helplessness, our weakness, our suffering, and transformed these things into the path to glory.

Within this tradition Teresa based her teaching on prayer on a personal love for Jesus, especially in the tangible aspects of his humanity: his human helplessness: crib, cross and Eucharist. In an era when the liturgy was a closed book to all except the educated she found ways to enliven devotion through re-enacting the stories attached to Bethlehem, Nazareth, Jerusalem and Carmel with her sisters. She chose St Joseph as her special patron since he was the man closest to Jesus on earth. Prayer, for Teresa, was to live with Jesus as friend and lover, everything directed away from self and towards him, his work, his glory, his church. 'Zeal' is one of the watchwords of Carmel and is an apt motto for Teresa just as it was for Elijah. Without zeal the Carmelite way of life has no meaning.

As Teresa explored the Order's beginnings she extracted the inner meaning of those early days, applying it to the women of her own culture and country, fashioning a lifestyle suitable for sixteenth-century Spain. She accepted women into her convents of modest means and a variety of temperaments and gifts. She renounced her family name and became plain Teresa of Jesus. To her, the summons to holiness was a clarion call that must not be denied or minimised in any way.

Teresa eschewed large monasteries for her nuns, instead favouring small, family-style groups with a common aim. Such a community did not need large, imposing buildings but could be established modestly in towns where people could support the nuns, their needs being so few. There would be no elaborate liturgy, no extensive property to maintain. Theirs was a 'hermit life' in the middle of the city.

However, Teresa did not take the original Rule literally and provide individual hermitages. While each sister had her own cell within the one house, the day was structured so as to provide alternation between solitude and community living in a fine balance.

Teresa viewed community life, not as an optional extra, but as an essential way to maturation, enabling a person to grow through interaction with others in self-knowledge and humility. Humility was a virtue she stressed constantly, the most needful virtue for those who practise prayer, for 'humility is truth'. Unless we live with others we can harbour many illusions about ourselves, as Teresa noted and described with gentle wit and teasing. Her hermit nuns were to be anything but isolates for she esteemed social qualities highly. 'Try, sisters, to be as agreeable as you can' she wrote in the *Way of Perfection*, 'so that others may like talking to you and not be put off by virtue. This is most important for nuns. The holier they are, the more sociable they should be with their sisters' (Ch. 24).

Another stricture was the common refectory enjoined by the Rule and long since neglected at the Incarnation. There, Teresa had witnessed the evils attendant on each nun providing for herself. Those who were poor often went hungry, others dined out with friends, others had food in plenty. Only recently a wall was pulled down for repairs in that convent to reveal the little private kitchen opening off Teresa's original cell and still redolent with the stale aroma of cooked food.

Teresa valued mutual support and encouragement among her sisters. Something completely her own was the introduction of a recreation period twice a day. These often rang with laughter, for Teresa was a great entertainer and would sing and dance with castanets, or write amusing verses to popular tunes.

Enclosure was Teresa's way of highlighting the eremitical spirit of Carmel. The sisters were to be wholly God-centred and this, in her estimation, demanded strict reclusion (although in reforming the friars she did not require this as part of their lifestyle; she expected them to continue with their apostolate of teaching and preaching which was closed to women). Teresa wanted her houses to be, and to be seen to be, deserts devoted to prayer. Yet her discipline was extremely gentle in practice. Surely the person who knows the vagaries of human nature is compassionate if she truly prays.

A very maternal woman herself, Teresa never underestimated the importance of a warm, happy environment where, in the manner of the early hermits, the nuns could live simply, pray, enjoy each other's company and work hard for a living. She was always willing to be patient, understanding of the gradualness of the growth process, attuned to human needs – had she not experienced her own frailty often enough? 'Do not trouble yourself in the least about how perfect she is', wrote Teresa to one of her prioresses worried about a nun's progress. 'It will be sufficient if she does what she can, as they say, and does not offend God. There is always a great deal to put up with, especially when one is beginning' (Letter 184).

As a woman, Teresa was notably interested in the place of women in the Church, which she contrasted with the place of women in the Gospels. She was convinced that, contrary to popular theories, women were called to the heights of holiness and, for her, the apostolate of holiness was the most meaningful apostolate of all. It was by meditating on the women depicted in the New Testament that Teresa developed her theories of close companionship with Christ, and she noted his compassion and understanding towards women which elicited from them such a warm response.

Always a relational person herself, Teresa scrutinised the interaction of women with the Lord and drew her own conclusions. In fact, what attracts Teresa most about Mary, what makes her love her as primary patron of the Order and exemplar of Carmelite life, is her deep bond with Christ as his mother and foremost disciple.

Other women who claimed her attention were those related to Jesus by ties of flesh – St Anne and St Merentiana, legendary names of his grandmother and great grandmother respectively, and those related to him by love, thus embodying some particular aspect of holiness. Such were the Magdalen who imaged conversion – the passage from sin to ardent love; the Samaritan woman who craved living water; and Martha, who by her good works prepared the ground for prayer and proved prayer's reality.

Remember that someone must cook the meals and count yourselves happy to be able to serve like Martha. Reflect that true humility consists to a great extent in being ready to do what the Lord desires to do with you, and happy that he should do it, and always considering yourselves unworthy to be his servants. If contemplation and mental and vocal prayer and tending the sick and serving in the house and working at even the lowliest tasks are of service to the Guest who comes to stay with us and eat with us and take his recreation with us, what should it matter to us if we do one of these things rather than another?

(*Way of Perfection*, Ch. 17)

Teresa's own exuberant style of prayer was supplemented by a very shrewd observation of her nuns as she exhorted them to live by the ideals she proposed. Her last twenty years were spent in founding convents, travelling, business negotiations, reforming the friars, coping with a possible split in the Order (which she did all in her power to deflect and which came about only after her death). Hers was a life fully active and fully contemplative.

In making foundations throughout Spain Teresa demonstrated her conviction that one holy person, one completely handed over to God that he may accomplish his will in her, is worth any number of mediocre Christians.

Yet Teresa also held firmly to the belief that, while she had a special role within the Carmelite Order, all were called to holiness. Her many letters testify to this as she exhorts relatives and friends of all sorts and conditions of life to persevere in the search for God in a spirit of discretion and gentleness, for he denies himself to no one who asks for the Living Water of prayer and union.

Teresa stressed the ordinary human virtues, not mystical experience, as the gauge of love. Prayer which does not issue in appropriate action is disguised selfishness. Love which remains unexpressed cannot be genuine love. In this vein she writes to her friend Fr Gratian:

> The fact is that, in these interior spiritual things, the most potent and acceptable prayer is the prayer that leaves the best effects. I do not mean it must immediately fill the soul with desires; for although such desires are good, they are sometimes not as good as our love of self makes us think. I should describe the best effects as those which are followed up by actions – when the soul not only desires the honour of God but really strives for it, and employs the memory and understanding in considering how it may please him and show its love for him more and more.
>
> Oh, that is real prayer – which cannot be said of a handful of consolations that do nothing but console ourselves. When the soul experiences these, they leave it weak and fearful, and sensitive to what others think about it. I should never want any prayer that would not make the virtues grow within me.
>
> (Letter 122)

There is no posing in Teresa. She is no 'saint' if by that we picture someone living with her head in the clouds. She is one of the most practical people to be met with anywhere in the annals of sanctity.

There are those who think that 'perfection' is something added on to the personality, warping natural growth, hedging one around with prohibitions and a stifling piety. The truth is that holiness can only be realised in the concrete. It wells up from the centre of the person, forming them in their own unique likeness to Christ, making them who they really are in the most secret core of their being. In the course of her development Teresa had to leave aside any preconceived ideas of sanctity that she might have fostered and find God in the story of her particular destiny. Holiness is not about being 'perfect' according to abstract norms. The saints can exhibit human weakness, misjudgements, misunderstandings about God and others. They have their limitations of time and place like the rest of us, for at the heart of holiness is not 'perfection' but surrender. It is the handing over of one's life to God, a continual listening to his demands, choosing him (not self) day in and day out in one's ordinary actions, thoughts and aspirations, and in this surrender finding one's true self and one's unique way to him.

Teresa wrote mainly at the request of her confessors who asked for an account of her life (this was written to placate the inquisitors, always wary of women 'mystics'). She wrote too to instruct her own nuns in the ways of prayer. Her writing is filled with imagery: the silkworm, the tortoise, the palmito, the castle, the butterfly. She writes in chatty, conversational style, something quite new in spiritual literature. Her *Life* is considered part of the literary heritage of Spain and she is one of that nation's chief patrons. Indeed, in the past, Spaniards and others went to great lengths to exalt Teresa's *limpia sangre* (pure blood), and cover up her Jewish origins.

Teresa rejoiced in extending what she loved to term 'Our Lady's Order'. Her devotion to Mary was tender and personal, just as it was to Mary's Son. As she entered the first house of the Reform in Avila she said it was as if she saw the Lord thanking her (Teresa) for 'all I had done for his mother'. That was sufficient reward. Her nuns were to live a Mary-life based on the hidden years at Nazareth – nothing spectacular,

just the daily struggle to love, to serve, to pray,
however the opportunity came to them.

> Take, O Lord, my loving heart;
> See, I yield it to thee whole,
> With my body, life and soul
> And my nature's every part.
> Sweetest Spouse, my life thou art;
> I have given myself to thee:
> What wilt thou have done with me?

> Let me live or let me die;
> Give me sickness, give me health;
> Give me poverty or wealth;
> Let me strive or peaceful lie,
> Weakness give or strength supply:
> I accept it all from thee;
> What wilt thou have done with me?

Death came to Teresa in old age, after many years of
activity and journeying. It was on the feast of St
Francis 1582 that she lay dying in the convent at Alba
de Tormes from a haemorrhage caused by an internal
cancer.

To the end she kept her consciousness. The priest
who brought Viaticum, one of her first friars,
approached with the Host. 'Now, my loving Lord, at
last it is time for us to see one another' she murmured.
This nun, so old and tired and sick, still preserved her
spark of youthful passion and familiarity with God.
Even before the final breath her humour reasserted
itself. Father Anthony, desiring to honour the putative
'saint', enquired pompously where she wished to be
buried. 'Good gracious' she cried, raising herself
slightly on her pillows 'Can you not spare me here a
little earth'. Then she lay back in the arms of her much

loved infirmarian, Anne of St Bartholomew and expired with a tiny sigh. It was over.

No one loved the Order more than Teresa did, and she specially loved the individual life spent pondering on the Law of the Lord, living always, like Elijah, in the presence of God. But she also relished community: the pleasures of friendship, of common celebrations, delight in creation. She was a woman of large heart; magnanimity was her outstanding trait. Nothing mean or petty deflected her from pursuing her goal.

Writing of Teresa, Louis Lavelle says:

> If we seek the essential features which distinguish this great saint, we shall find that she excelled in resolution and daring. She derived all her strength, confidence and zest, all her inflexible resolution in time of trial and danger, from her constant sense of the presence of God. No one knew better than she how to combine boldness in idea, hazard in enterprise, prudence and patience in execution. Listen to her cry; 'One may die, to be sure, but be defeated – never!' She was prepared to meet every challenge ... She never refused any task on the grounds of her own weakness, for if God required her to do it she knew he would give her the strength to carry it through.[1]

There could be no better tribute to Teresa than this, except perhaps the words of the Augustinian friar, Luis de Leon. Writing to Mother Anne of Jesus, one of Teresa's collaborators and then prioress of the Carmel of Madrid, he declared that, though he had not known Mother Teresa in the flesh, he saw her continually alive in both her daughters and her books. These were, and are, living images of herself and faithful witnesses to her sanctity. Thus Teresa lives on.

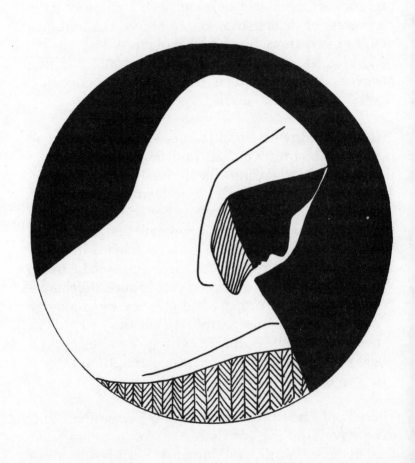

CHAPTER TEN

FRIAR JOHN – MYSTICAL DOCTOR

John of the Cross – the very name seems to arouse mixed feelings. Here is one of the great mystics; but so much of what people think about John is based on misconceptions about his teaching, arising from hearsay, or isolated sayings taken out of context.

The first misconception seems to be that John has nothing to say to those engaged in the active apostolate because he led an enclosed, contemplative life remote from the hurly-burly of current events. Nothing could be further from the truth. John was certainly contemplative by temperament but not by lifestyle. He was not a monk but a friar with a taxing ministry of teaching and preaching, involving him in a wide variety of relationships with both men and women. His life was not passed in an enclosure that secreted him from secular life.

John had close contacts with the universities of his day and was educated at the university of Salamanca, currently considered on a par with the seats of learning in Paris and Oxford. He undertook among his other duties the direction of laypeople. As a religious superior he supervised a great deal of building. He had to travel, organise studies for students, and he was caught up in the power politics of his own Order, in which he became an unwilling pawn and eventually a victim. John certainly knew all about the difficulties of combining prayer with ministry.

Another misconception is that John writes for advanced mystics and specialises in analysing rare mystical phenomena. These phenomena are applicable only to professionals in the highest states of prayer. Wrong again.

One of John's major works *The Living Flame of Love* was written for a married laywoman friend. His other books, though mainly addressed to the friars and nuns of his Order, treat of the most basic principles of the spiritual life. He has no time for so-called 'mystical phenomena', and advises his readers to disregard them all – to take no notice whatever of visions, locutions and similar things. The only sure basis of the spiritual life is Christ and the Gospels, for in the Son the Father has spoken his definitive word to humanity. To seek for some other private revelation is an insult to the Deity. In fact, far from exalting an other-worldly approach to life, John is primarily concerned with his readers becoming fully human and Christian as sons and daughters of God. Hence his teaching is relevant to everyone.

Further, it is thought by many that John is anti-creation, anti-human relationships, anti-pleasure. This too is a misconception. John had a real love for nature. He enjoyed a variety of deeply emotional human relationships, and he knew how to find pleasure in simple things. He says explicitly that creation is a mirror reflecting the Creator. But he also emphasises that all natural reality points beyond itself to God. Lasting joy can only be ours if we avoid enslavement to the temporal. This teaching is not peculiar to John although it is he who articulates it most strongly. All spiritual masters say the same thing in one way or another, including Francis of Assisi. Christianity is not essentially a nature religion. It draws its meaning from the cross of Christ and demands true self-denial if we are to discover the full life and freedom Jesus promised.

John is not some theorist whose doctrine has nothing specifically Christian about it. He does not lead us into a world of 'nothingness' but into a world where we find Christ. His teaching has no meaning when divorced from the Church and the Gospels. Faith in Jesus as Lord, faith in the whole Christian tradition, is the bedrock on which is built everything John has to say:

> There is no progess but in the imitation of Christ, who is the Way, the Truth and the Life, and the Gate by which whosoever will be saved must enter. Every spirit therefore that would walk in sweetness and ease, shunning the imitation of Christ is, in my opinion, worth nothing.
>
> Your first care must be lovingly and anxiously to endeavour to seek Christ in earnest in all your actions; doing every one of them to the uttermost of your power as Our Lord himself would have done them.
>
> (Maxims)

John takes for granted that the people he is writing for are living a committed Christian, sacramental life. He stresses over and over again that the Father has revealed all through the Son and that any counsel he, John, gives regarding the denial of the senses must never be extended to the sacred humanity on which we must meditate constantly. Jesus is the one to keep before our inner eye.

John is a true and uncompromising guide. His approach is not to get people feeling good about themselves but to face up to the truth. 'The truth will make you free', whereas we are caught up in all kinds of illusions that entangle us in misery. John bases his teaching on the theological virtues, faith, hope, and lovel; but especially faith:

> Because it is the function of the theological virtues to withdraw the soul from all that is less than God, it is theirs also to unite it with him.
>
> Without walking in the practice of these three virtues it is impossible to attain to perfect love of God.
>
> The way of the faith is sound and safe, and along this way souls must journey from virtue to virtue.
>
> (Maxims)

The motivation of a person; the faith, hope and love of God with which actions are performed, matters more than the acquisition of moral virtues or the perfect performance of religious duties.

Within the Order, the two best known modern Carmelites, Thérèse of Lisieux and Elizabeth of the Trinity, testified that they found in John of the Cross their surest guide – the guide of faith, not religious sentiment. Both were living perfectly ordinary lives devoid of mystical phenomena. What distinguished them was the ardour with which they lived their faith in darkness, the depths of motivation provided by their love of the person of Christ, and the hope that God would fulfil all their desires if they trusted themselves utterly to him.

Another writer, the French philosopher Alain Cugno, has recently published a book examining

John from a philosophical viewpoint. He acknowledges that John has a unique grasp of human nature and its fulfilment. Ruth Burrows, one of today's most respected spiritual guides, relies heavily on John of the Cross. Her book *Ascent to Love* was reviewed in the *Times* as a significant contribution to ecumenical dialogue. John's doctrine is applicable not only to all Christians but, as Cugno says so succinctly, to all human beings. And psychologists have reiterated what John knew many years ago: that we are caught up and entangled in webs of non-freedom through all kinds of addictive behaviour patterns which must be addressed if we are to reach wholeness.

Like everyone else John was not born a saint. He had to grow and be formed by his life experience. He had to develop humanly, spiritually, emotionally; and though, unlike St Teresa, he does not write autobiographically, what he says is obviously influenced by his personal history.

John de Ypes was born in 1542, the youngest of three boys in a very poor (almost indigent) family. His father came from the moneyed class and had been a reasonably well-off merchant. However, on a business trip to Fontiveros he met and fell in love with Catalina, a young orphan woman, a cloth weaver with a tragic background. It was rumoured that her father had been burned at the stake either as a Judaiser or a Moor; so besides her poverty she was the bearer of a social stigma. Catalina was the kind of woman that no one who was anyone wanted to know.

Gonzalo, John's father, nevertheless resolved to marry the woman to whom he had given his heart. He was forthwith ostracised by his family. This was disastrous as it deprived the couple of the network of extended family and friends considered indispensable for life in society.

In this case love was stronger than social estrangement. Gonzalo and Catalina were wed and strove to bring up their children on a pittance, earned by piecework weaving in their own home.

John was the child of a love match, most unusual for his day. Yet he saw that faithful commitment to love could be extremely costly, bringing suffering in its train. When John writes of love it is well to have his own background in mind. He himself was a loved and wanted child, but he could see that the path of love was far from easy when followed with fidelity to choices made in the first rush of emotion.

Gonzalo, weakened by unaccustomed manual work and material hardship, died after a long illness when John was seven. Catalina, left completely alone to support her sons, was to prove herself one of Spain's strong women. The second son Louis, died of malnutrition and Catalina decided to move to the city of Medina del Campo, a well-known centre of international commerce, where she hoped work would be available.

John was enrolled at a school for poor boys where he received a rudimentary education. He had already been apprenticed unsuccessfully to several craftsmen in an effort to have him earn money to contribute to the support of his family.

In the end John managed to find employment at a local hospital while he continued his studies at the newly founded Jesuit college. The hospital, needless to say, was not like our contemporary sterile glasshouses. Medina, a commercial city, harboured much of the dregs of Spanish cosmopolitan society (among whom was John himself). As a hospital orderly in a place euphemistically termed 'for those suffering from contagious diseases' he was actually nursing paupers who had contracted syphillis and other related venereal infections. He did this without conveying any sense of disgust at the dressing of terrible sores. He was a gifted and sensitive nurse, never seeming to pass moral judgement on those he cared for. He was even willing to beg in the public market for the support of his patients.

John's background could hardly have contrasted more with that of St Teresa and most others who entered the religious life. He had literally been 'at the bottom of the pile' during his youth.

The patron of the hospital was keen for John to proceed to priestly ordination so that he could continue with a spiritual ministry to the patients as chaplain. Instead, for unknown reasons, John decided to enter the Carmelite Order which had a friary in the city. He was twenty-one.

John began his religious life with great zeal. He was fortunate to have been accepted at all despite his good record in studies. Time proved him to be a brilliant student. He studied at the university of Salamanca where some of the most advanced learning of the day was taught under internationally recognised professors.

But in the community John was not particularly popular. He was overly serious (due in part to his lack of a carefree childhood) and very penitential. His piety was strained and he tended to judge harshly those who did not come up to his exacting standards. Many young people start out like this in seminaries and religious houses. The views of novices are apt to be narrow as they resolve to embrace standards impossible to maintain. One admires their earnestness, but if they are to develop as they should this stage has to be outgrown to make room for a broader, more humane outlook. And John did grow, fortunately for him and for Carmel as a whole.

While being somewhat narrow to begin with, John was truly set upon a God-centred life. It is important, too, to remember that his ability to bear hardship was ingrained from childhood and could not be the common standard required for those coming from a more comfortable background. In fact, John began to keep the Carmelite Rule without mitigation on his own initiative, going barefoot, fasting, spending periods in solitude.

Just before ordination John was considering a transfer to the Carthusian Order, where he felt that his attraction to prayer would have fuller scope, when a providential meeting took place. He was twenty-five when, in Medina del Campo, a friend introduced him to a remarkable woman already being widely talked about in Spain – the fifty-two year old Madre Teresa of Jesus, then at the height of her powers. She was in Medina to establish another convent of nuns following her Reform.

John was presented to *La Madre* and she immediately recognised the great potential hidden under an unprepossessing exterior. John was small, prematurely bald, overly serious. She was vivacious, expansive, physically attractive, gifted on many levels. She had recently obtained permission to found a house of reformed friars and saw John as the ideal collaborator.

Having kissed the Spanish equivalent of the Blarney stone, Teresa quickly squashed John's Carthusian aspirations and assured him that he could find fulfilment in his own Order if he would listen to her and undertake the new project she had in mind. Besides, the Church needed apostles and good priests; she would show him how to become one as a Carmelite. So began the friendship between Teresa and John. John was to be the first friar member of the

Reform, and for him Teresa always retained a special affection.

Teresa had the unusual gift of being both a man's woman and a woman's woman. 'We women' she confides intimately as she addresses her nuns. 'I write to my daughters, they will understand me as women understand each other's language'. But she teases an overconfident priest in these words: 'We women are not so easy to understand as you think. You hear our confession and feel you have got us taped. There is more to us than that.' Yet Teresa was also a man's woman, evoking admiration from the male sex for her administrative and organising abilities. She knew how to butter men up so that they felt they were in charge when really it was she who was calling the tune. She was able to relate to men as a friend and equal, very unusual in the world of the Counter-Reformation. She let men feel marvellous about themselves – a great gift in a talented feminist.

John himself was never a great leader. By temperament he was gentle, with a tender, compassionate side, evident in his talent for nursing and his romantic poetry (which contrasts favourably with Teresa's doggerel verses). Teresa revered John's sanctity rather than his leadership qualities. He was solid and devoted rather than charismatic.

So John joined the Reform and gave his life to its ideals henceforth. In Carmel he rediscovered the contemplative dimension of his vocation with its hermit spirituality; but he managed to meld this with commitment to the apostolate. Instead of the Carthusian life which may well have fed his desire for reclusion in an unhealthy way, he blossomed and grew from many new contacts, especially with the nuns. John's friendship with Anne of Jesus could rank with that of any between the great saints like Francis and

Clare, Francis de Sales and Jane de Chantal, Diana and Jordan of Saxony. He was renowned for his sensitivity and non-judgmentalness which ensured he was in great demand as a confessor and preacher.

Meanwhile, John's former brethren were intensely jealous as the Reform expanded, feeling that it was a threat to the Order's unity. John was kidnapped and spirited away to the friary of Toledo where he was held incommunicado in solitary confinement. Filthy, locked in a space that had once been a cupboard, he was threatened with perpetual incarceration unless he deserted the Reform. Twice a week he had to undergo a scourging in the refectory, the scars of which he bore for the rest of his life.

Feeling completely isolated and forgotten by his friends, John knew that unless he escaped he would die. One night, after careful planning, he managed to let himself down from a window in another room, using strips of blanket he had knotted together to form a rope. Dropping the last few feet in the darkness he ran to a nearby convent where the nuns speedily hid him from his pursuers. This escape is the basis of John's best known poem, the *Dark Night*, symbol of the soul's costly journey through darkness to the joy of union with God:

> Upon a darksome night,
> Kindling with love in flame of yearning keen,
> O moment of delight!
> I went by all unseen,
> New hushed to rest the house where I had been.

Teresa was delighted to have John back. She had been nearly out of her mind with worry and was horrified to hear what had happened to him in his imprisonment. 'He was not even allowed to change his shirt!'

she exclaimed, as if this was one of his worst sufferings. Teresa was known for her love of cleanliness and order in all things!

The remainder of John's life was spent in various posts in the Order, especially in the formation of students and the spiritual direction of nuns. Many of his confrères had differing ideas on how the Reform should develop and they fought for power and influence in quite scandalous ways. John seems to have been caught between two factions: those who emphasised prayer and retirement to the exclusion of all activity, wanting a literal imitation of the first hermits; and those who pressed for expansion into a variety of missionary projects.

John was an authentic interpreter of the Carmelite charism in that he saw that a balance between solitude and action was to be maintained despite the ever-recurrent temptation to cut tensions and follow one or other path to the exclusion of its opposite. A suitable apostolate for the Carmelite guarantees the original purity of the ideal. Prayer and ministry are interrelated. To abandon the apostolate would be to invite a formalistic cultivation of solitude for its own sake. To neglect prayer in favour of activity alone is a betrayal of the contemplative spirit that should animate all work.

John, trying to implement this vision, was scorned by fanatics on both sides. When his enemies came into power he was gradually forced out of all posts of importance and sent to southern Spain under an unfriendly superior. There he died, sick and excommicate (though fortunately the decree had not reached him in time and he received the Sacraments and honourable burial). His whole life had been dedicated to an ideal which in so many ways seemed a failure as far as the friars were concerned. Yet of them all he was the one who best understood and lived the charism of Carmel.

As a writer, John's books are mainly commentaries on his poems. He ranks as a major Spanish poet despite his small output. The commentaries were written later for people who asked what the poems meant, when most likely he would have preferred to let the poetry speak for itself. Unlike Teresa, John expounds the principles and theory of the spiritual life when he writes. His treatises are dry, not racily autobiographical like those of his mentor.

However, like all writers, John could not help being influenced by his historical circumstances and personal experience. In stressing love as the supreme motivational force, he had before him the example of his own parents and his personal fidelity, through thick and thin, to an Order which crucified him. For John, love was a costly business, a commitment to hold firm to, whatever transpired: 'to have and to hold for better for worse, for richer for poorer, in sickness and in health'.

John is not a man of practical expediency but of principles deeply held and adherred to. He knew how to be faithful in the face of grave misunderstanding and outright persecution. Witness his words to a friend as he faced exile and disgrace:

Jesus be in your soul. Trouble not yourself my daughter about what concerns me, since it troubles me not at all. The only thing which grieves me is to see the blame laid on those to whom it does not belong. For the Author of these things is not man but God, who knows what is best for us, and orders all things for our greater good.

Think of this only, that all is ordained by God. And do you love where there is no love and you will draw love out. May His Majesty preserve you and make you grow in his love.

(Letter 16)

From John love is the *leitmotiv* of everything. Love obtains all. Thus. 'one instant of pure love is more profitable for the Church and the world than all good actions put together, though it seem that nothing were done'.

Love and fidelity are inseparable. To go on loving, no matter what, is the true test of devotion. If we genuinely want God and try to love him we shall have him, adverse external circumstances notwithstanding:

> Some there are who call the Bridegroom their Beloved, but he is not really beloved because their heart is not wholly with him. Their prayers, therefore, are not effectual with God, and they shall not obtain their petitions until, persevering in prayer, they fix their minds upon God and their hearts wholly in loving affection upon him; for nothing can be obtained from God but by love.
>
> This is therefore the test to discern the true lovers of God. Are they satisfied with anything less than God? For the heart cannot be satisfied with possessions, but rather in detachment from all things and poverty of spirit.

(*Spiritual Canticle*, Stanza 1)

Fidelity equals practical faith. Faith is the choice to love God above all, to want him alone as our ultimate fulfilment. In John's teaching we encounter God by faith. By faith we are drawn into a love relationship with a God whom we cannot see or experience through the senses.

John does not treat of dogmas and doctrines, he takes for granted that his readers are Catholic Christians. Faith for him is not primarily about dogmas, it is a personal assent to the God revealed in Scripture and tradition, a casting of oneself in love upon the mystery of God, abandoning self with absolute trust, in union with Christ in his passion. This is the way of darkness, because God cannot be understood or grasped by our finitude.

The dark nights are really nothing other than the growth process by which the ego is ever more deeply purified, allowing the true self to emerge, cleansed of all selfishness and self-seeking. Only when selfish desires cease (the theme of the *Ascent of Mount Carmel*) will we stop acting from motives of covetousness and self-glorification and find true peace, lasting joy.

Desires hold back and enslave the heart, like a dog running to and fro on a chain, or a bird restrained from flight by a single thread. It is because we do not see God, feel God, that it is costly to choose in darkness, really believing that, if we do, we will find freedom and fulfilment.

Do we want to be free of our addictions and compulsions? Are we ready to sustain our faithfulness when the thrill of emotion wears off? John never ceases challenging us, asking awkward questions, probing our desires. These questions cause us to search our hearts and beg for grace. But it is precisely in our hearts that we find the God who seems to elude us. He is not far away; he is so close that we are blinded by his very nearness.

God is joy, peace, everything we can desire. All we have to do is clear away the debris and he fills the emptiness. So John can cry out in amazement:

O soul, most beautiful of creatures, who so earnestly longs to know the place where your Beloved is, that you may seek him and be united to him. You are yourself the very tabernacle where he dwells, the secret chamber of his retreat where he is hidden. Rejoice therefore and exult, because all your good and all your hope is so near you as to be within you. Yes, rather rejoice that you cannot be without it, for lo 'the kingdom of God is within you'. So says the Bridegroom himself, and his servant St Paul adds: 'You are the temple of the living God'. What joy for the soul to learn that God never abandons it even in mortal sin, how much less in a state of grace? What more can you desire, what more can you seek outside, seeing that within you you have your riches, your delight, your Beloved whom you seek and desire.

(*Spiritual Canticle*, Stanza 1)

And who is the one who brings us the Lord, the Beloved? It is the Virgin of Carmel who is coming to us long before we have gone out to her, and who looks only for a place to rest so that she can bring her Son to birth within us:

With the divinest Word, the Virgin
Made pregnant, down the road
Comes walking, if you'll grant her
A room in your abode.

EPILOGUE

Therefore, behold, I will allure her,
and bring her into the wilderness and speak
   tenderly to her.
And there she shall answer as in the days of her
   youth,
as at the time when she came out of the land of
   Egypt.
And I will betroth you to me forever;
I will betroth you to me in righteousness and
   justice,
in steadfast love and in mercy.
I will betroth you to me in faithfulness;
and you shall come to know the Lord.
                     (Hosea 22:14, 15b, 19–20)

This well known passage from the prophet Hosea is one of the readings assigned as a possible choice for a Mass celebrating a Jubilee of Religious Profession. But it omits the first part of verse 15 which actually gives the piece its full significance: 'There I will give her her vineyards and make the valley of Achor (Trouble Valley) a door of hope.' This refers to an incident recounted in the book of Joshua (Jos.

7:22–26) where a great pile of stones was raised at the
very entrance to the Promised Land, commemorating
a sin of covetousness and ensuring it would never be
forgotten – the stones would be for an everlasting
memorial of Israel's infidelity, a warning to successive generations.

Hosea, however, has the Lord assure Israel that this
incident of shame is precisely what will be transformed into a doorway of hope. Recognised,
acknowledged and remembered 'Trouble Valley'
opens Israel to God's mercy. The stones remind her of
her election, and God promises her a new, permanent
union rising from the very ruins of the first.

When I began to write this book I was remember-
ing myself as a girl of fourteen approaching the
Carmel of Holy Hope. I felt quite ready then for
whatever it would cost to follow a vocation. But I was
not in any way prepared for my own Valley of Achor.
The journey that each of us makes to the Land that is
Carmel is a journey that has to pass through shame
and failure and human neediness, however much we
may desire to bypass these things and attain the
Promised Land without suffering. True hope is only
possible when we have faced near despair and
allowed God to lead us through it to new life.

The history of the Carmelite Order has not been
without its share of infidelity, of obscurity, of times
when sacrifice rather than mercy prevailed. This
should engender in us a basic humility; a realisation
that God's covenant does not depend on our worthi-
ness. It depends on his choice and his loving kindness.

My visit to Aylesford was a moment of grace and
insight, perhaps the only one I have ever known in
my life, when I could put a finger on what I thought
was an open wound and realise that only a scar
remained. I had been in contact all along with an

unobtrusive Presence that was nothing other than the healing acceptance and love of God. It had always been there of course but I could not be conscious of it. My heart was blocked, as was the Valley of Achor, by a great pile of stones.

Life can have its high points, its fleeting glimpses of something that transcends time and place; but day to day living in the land of Carmel still has to be worked out in one's familiar, constrained environment.

So what has it meant for *me* to 'live Carmel'? Over the years as an enclosed nun it has meant nothing spectacular. It has meant simply getting up daily at 5.30 a.m. for another round of alternating prayer and work, no matter how I have felt. It has meant drawing strength daily from the Mass and the Eucharistic Presence. It has meant sharing the lot of many who find life wearisome, who find it hard to believe in a hidden, caring God when their human trust has been shattered and betrayed. It has meant going on when I felt I could not go on; acknowledging my weakness to myself and others.

But it has also meant being with a supportive community which has accepted and challenged me. It has meant putting myself aside for the welfare of others, letting my heart be dilated in order to give and receive love in the kind of family-community Teresa had in mind when she founded the discalced nuns. It has meant cooking and cleaning, caring for the sick and the novices, a bit of writing and drawing ... It has meant meals and celebrations, frustrating incomprehension and points of contact. It has meant shouldering my own share of solitude and loneliness, labour and tears, while I, like the biblical Ruth have gleaned in my life for the bits and pieces that no one else wanted, gathering up fragments so that nothing was wasted – all given to God with a joyful heart.

For many years I have had on the door of my cell a reproduction of Millet's painting of *The Gleaners*. It depicts women together in a field. They are plain peasant women, distinguished only by their heavy clogs. They are totally without glamour, totally unselfconscious as, with bent backs, they search the ground for stray stalks of wheat. This they will use to mill and bake the bread of the poor, bread that will nourish themselves and their children.

Over the years I have been like those women, struggling to make sense of a life seemingly wasted on the outward level. I entered religious life very young, before any other life could take hold of me. I retreated from 'the world' because I was frightened of myself and my feelings. I thought something outside myself, some tested structure and spirituality would offer me safety and provide me with answers, give me a name and an identity. And in coming to Carmel I tried to ensure I was even safer, behind an even more secure barricade.

But fortunately for me, as I see it now, things did not work out so smoothly. I experienced a deep alienation from myself no matter how much I tried to fit into the proper pattern. I was without any sense of integrity because my heart was not in tune with reality, the reality of my own weakness, and I could not love what I hated and despised.

I am learning now that I can only be humanly myself; that what I am in myself is my only gift, and that my poverty opens me to God's mercy. What I thought would be a safe, straightforward, domestic life has been one where I have been ultimately challenged to grow and face areas of life I wanted to suppress: my inner violence, my bitterness, my selfishness. In this way I have been led to trust in the mercy and grace of God who has brought me to the

Land of Carmel in order to teach me to be human. My
ideal self has had to give way before the forces within
that struggle to nurture a particular life, thrusting up
from the roots of neediness to flower in freedom.

Only God can demolish the protective walls that
surround us, enabling us to embrace the world and
others unshielded by illusion.

> Jerusalem will be inhabited as villages without
> walls because of the multitude of people and
> animals in her. For I will be a wall of fire round
> about her, says the Lord, and I will be the glory
> within her.
>
> (Zech. 2:4–5)

One of the themes of the Book of Ruth is that of
teshuva, the Hebrew word for repentance or return.
Teshuva is a process that seizes upon hope, affirms life
and moves towards redemption. It is a process that
unfolds as Ruth and Naomi move together from
Moab and Judah. It is a journey that means different
things for each woman but which neither could make
alone. It is a journey through loss and grief to new life
and a distinctive harvest for each one: for Ruth fruitfulness and love in a home of her own; for Naomi
release from bitterness and the joy of a grandchild
who will be an ancestor of David and, through him,
of the promised Messiah.

The bond which unites the main characters in the
story, Naomi, Ruth and Boaz, is a love springing from
mutual respect, a capacity for commitment and
friendship, a willingness to attend to the voice of the
Lord in a setting where human choice and divine
destiny are interwoven as in a seamless garment.

It is within the ambience combining human
circumstances and divine law that God empowers

Ruth to take hold of her own destiny and risk herself in the gift of herself. She is enabled to be fruitful, not so that she can be exalted in her own eyes, but so that the story of God's people and land can be continued through her self-donation. In the same way, the child she bears is not hers alone, but is destined to become a blessing for all Israel.

Mary herself must often have read and pondered the story of Ruth. Her Son was Ruth's descendant born, as was Obed, in Bethlehem of Judah. Maybe, in the days of her widowhood, Mary too had to glean with the poor, like the women in Millet's picture; immersing herself in a society where she passed unnoticed, living with life's contradictions so as to discover the divine hand guiding her to fulfilment.

Carmel is that place where I can truly become who I am called to be – not without struggle, not without human help, for it is always a struggle to love. The final goal of the Promised Land is not reached in this life except in one's imagination. We have to live in the continuous process of repentance. This becomes a reality only if I face the jealousy, the unkindness, the impatience, the conceit within myself, and journey with them in order to emerge, if not into the light, then into the shadow of God's wings, symbolised in the garments of Boaz spread over the woman he finds lying at his feet in the silence of the night.

St John of the Cross, in his celebrated *Prayer of the Enamoured Soul* ends with these words: 'I will draw near to you in silence and uncover your feet, that you may unite me to yourself, making my soul your bride. O my God, I beseech you, leave me not for a moment, for I know not the value of my soul.' We can never really know our value, for our redemption has been paid for by the blood of the Lamb 'without blemish or spot' (I Pet. 1:9).

It is good to be aware of our blemishes, holding this awareness in tension with the truth that, blemishes notwithstanding, we have been gratuitously loved and redeemed. If that truth enters our consciousness we will not only value ourselves aright but we will be impelled to love others, insofar as we can, with a reflection of the love of God, offered and made tangible through human relationships.

I could have written more on Carmel's history – on Thérèse of Lisieux, Elizabeth of the Trinity, Edith Stein, Titus Brandsma and others – but I have chosen to end with Teresa and John because, once the foundations of a charism are laid, it is for each one to make it their own. Each one has to communicate the charism to a new generation through the love and creative fidelity each offers to the others in a common search for truth. To be ready to stand undefended, 'unwalled', is the only possible way to dwell fruitfully in Mary's land, keeping Jesus company in prayer, being poor with and among the poor.

If I had not experienced human love and been helped to open myself to it I would have remained forever the 'outsider'. But in Carmel there is room enough for everyone. God in his Providence finds ways to touch the human heart, to dispel bitterness, to make it possible to find the seedlings of life hidden among all that seems to be dead and lost. Even the most fragile green shoot is worthwhile, precious, and to be nurtured with care.

Carmel is not an environment above and beyond the human; a place which offers an angelic existence. Rather it is a place where the human story of each one is touched by the loving kindness and mercy of God. I hope this process has begun for me; and I hope and pray that others too, whatever their inner darkness, will come to realise that God's love is stronger than all the evil within and without, of which we are so afraid. Indeed, we can feel so overwhelmed that we never really have the courage to live; and that is the greatest tragedy.

Mary as mother symbolises the Lord's mercy and graciousness, compassion and tenderness. The Land of Carmel should do likewise, not because the weakness and sinfulness of those who live there is ignored or suppressed, but because there it can encounter the love of Christ which proves itself to be the stronger force. In the adventure of traversing the Land of Carmel, in whatever way is our particular vocation, we journey together through repentance and loss to the joy of redemption.

There is another aspect of the Order's history that needs to be explored more deeply. What does it mean to grow and to change as a living organism? If the Order is to speak to today's world and the present needs of humanity what is being asked *now* in the way of realistic self-appraisal and self-sacrifice? It is no good thinking we are embodying timeless values if we are perceived as just being out of date.

Discernment is a delicate process which can only spring from closeness to Jesus in prayer. It has to take account of our human needs as well as our vocation to witness to the all-sufficiency of God. The witness depends upon men and women of Carmel today being unafraid to search their hearts and then *choose life*, with all its attendant risks.

In a homily at the closing of an international gathering of Teresian Carmelite friars in 1995, Fr Camillo Maccise, Superior General, challenged the participants to reflect on Jesus' invitation to Peter after the Resurrection 'When you were young you fastened your belt and walked where you wished. But when you are old you will stretch out your hands and someone else will fasten a belt around you and take you where you would rather not go' (John 21:18). In commenting on these words Fr Camillo says:

> Talking to Peter after the Resurrection, Jesus makes him understand that, in spite of his desire to organise his life and arrange everything, there will be circumstances in which he will be forced to do certain things which probably he would never have even thought of.[1]

The same thing happens in individual lives and the life of an Order. At the beginning of a vocation or a particular charism the way ahead may seem clearly defined. But with the passing of time new situations arise which require us to take up, as Peter had to do, and as Mary before him, unforseen and unimagined challenges, unimagined journeying and suffering, so as to come to a maturer joy in the knowledge that '*All is grace*', as Thérèse of Lisieux could say at the end of her life.

For myself, since writing this account of Carmel's history and spirituality I have been able to move to Aylesford and make it my home. I have come here to be a praying presence in the midst of people, to be with them where they are, to use my experience of enclosed life in a more 'open' manner. I am choosing to walk a new way along age-old paths, in the confidence that in Carmel's land there is a place for me also, as for all others who are on this common journey of search and surrender.

In that journey we walk with the Carmelite saints and sinners that make up our common history. We have the inspiring figure of the prophet Elijah, and the companionship of Mary, Jesus' mother and ours. She has been given to us in Carmel as mother, sister and friend. Most especially I feel her presence here at her own shrine in Aylesford, the place where the Rule was finalised and adapted for Europe, and where she is honoured in the glory of her Assumption by thousands of pilgrims every year.

The lot marked out me me is my delight,
welcome indeed the heritage that falls to me.

(Ps. 16:16)

Feast of Our Lady of Sion
January 20th 1999

Notes

Chapter 2. Time and Place

1. Nicholas of Narbonne, *The Flaming Arrow* (trans. M. Edwards) Teresian Press, 1985, p. 43.

Chapter 4. From East to West

1. Nicholas of Narbonne, op. cit., pp. 29–30.
2. Ibid., p.43.

Chapter 5. The Spirit of Elijah

1. G. Barry, *Historical Notes on the Carmelite Order*, Private printing, undated, p. 17.
2. *Book of the Institution of the First Monks*, chs 1–9, (trans. M. Edwards), private printing, 1969, ch. 2.

Chapter 6. Mary – Lady of the Place

1. Henri Focillon, *The Art of the West II Gothic*, Phaidon, 1963, p. 72.
2. D. Nicholl, *The Testing of Hearts*, Lamp Press, 1989, p. 305.

3. From 'The Astronomical Calendar of Nicholas of Lynn 1386', quoted in *Carmelite Digest*, Spring 1996, p. 30.

Chapter 7. The Advent of the Nuns

1. R. Southern, *Western Society and the Church in the Middle Ages*, Penguin, 1970, p. 317.

Chapter 8. Clothing and Contemplation for All

1. Scholem Asch, *Mary* (trans. Leo Steinberg), Macdonald, 1950, p. 425.
2. H. M. Robinson, *The Cardinal*, Macdonald, 1951, pp. 227–228.
3. Ibid., p. 229.

Chapter 9. La Madre

1. L. Lavelle, *The Meaning of Holiness*, Burns and Oates, 1951, p. 84.

Epilogue

1. Address to the General Definitory, April 1995, published by SIC.

BIBLIOGRAPHY

Barry G., *Historical Notes on the Carmelite Order*, Private printing, undated

Bouyer L., *Introduction to Spirituality*, DLT, 1961

Brueggemann, W., *The Land*, Fortess Press, 1977

Burrows R., *Ascent to Love*, DLT, 1987

Cugno, A., *St John of the Cross*, trans. B. Wall, Burns and Oates, 1982

Edwards M., *Introduction to the Rule of St Albert*, Private printing, 1973

—— *The Book of the Institution of the First Monks, Chs 1–9*, Private printing, 1969

Elizabeth of the Trinity *Complete Works*, trans A. E. Nash, ICS Publications, 1995

Fielding E., *Courage to Build Anew*, Burns and Oates, 1968

Focillon H., *The Art of the West II Gothic*, Phaidon Press, 1963

Friedman E., *The Latin Hermits of Mount Carmel*, Carmelite Press, 1979

Hinnebusch P., *Jesus and Elijah*, Servant Books, 1978

John of the Cross *Collected Works*, trans. D. Lewis, Longman Green, 1864

Lavelle L., *The Meaning of Holiness*, Burns and Oates, 1954

Lawrence C. H., *Medieval Monasticism*, Longmans, 1984

Merton T., *The Power and Meaning of Love*, Sheldon Press, 1953

Minogue C., *Carmel is All Mary's*, Private printing, 1965

Morton H. V., *In the Steps of the Master*, Methuen & Co., 1934

Nicholas of Narbonne, *The Flaming Arrow*, trans. M. Edwards, Teresian Press, 1985

Powicke M., *The Thirteenth Century*, Oxford, Clarendon Press, 1962

Smet J., *The Carmelites Vol. 1*, Institutum Carmelitarum, 1975

—— *Cloistered Carmel*, Institutum Carmelitarum, 1986

Southern R., *Western Society and the Church in the Middle Ages*, Penguin, 1970

Stuart D., *Men and Women of Plantagenet England*, Harrap & Co., 1932

Roth C., *A Short History of the Jewish People*, Oxford Press, 1935

Teresa St., *Collected Works and Letters*, Trans. E. Allison Peers, Sheed and Ward, 1946